Public Relations
for Pharmacists

Notice

The author and the publisher have made every effort to ensure the accuracy and completeness of the information presented in this book. However, the author and the publisher cannot be held responsible for the continued currency of the information, any inadvertent errors or omissions, or the application of this information. Therefore, the author and the publisher shall have no liability to any person or entity with regard to claims, loss, or damage caused or alleged to be caused, directly or indirectly, by the use of information contained herein.

Public Relations for Pharmacists

Tina L. Pugliese, APR
Director of Public Relations
American Pharmaceutical Association
Washington, D.C.

American Pharmaceutical Association
Washington, D.C.

APhA

Acquiring Editor: Julian I. Graubart
Substantive Editor: Linda R. Harteker
Copyeditor: L. Luan Corrigan
Layout and Graphics: Claire Purnell Graphic Design
Cover Designer: Mary Jane Hickey
Proofreader: Kathleen K. Wolter
Indexer: Lillian R. Rodberg

© 2000 by the American Pharmaceutical Association
Published by the American Pharmaceutical Association
2215 Constitution Avenue, N.W.
Washington, DC 20037-2985
www.aphanet.org

Library of Congress Cataloging-in-Publication Data
Pugliese, Tina L.
    Public relations for pharmacists / Tina L. Pugliese.
      p. ; cm.
    Includes index.
    ISBN 1-58212-011-0 (softbound)
      1. Pharmacy–Public relations. I. American Pharmaceutical Association. II. Title.
    [DNLM: 1. Pharmacy Administration. 2. Pharmacists–organization & administration.
  3. Public Relations. QV 737 P978p 2000]
  RS56 .P84 2000
  615.1'068'8–dc21
                                                                                    00-038958

How to Order This Book
By phone: 800-878-0729 (802-862-0095 from outside the United States)
VISA®, MasterCard®, and American Express® cards accepted.

Dedication

To Mom with much love and thanks for all your support.

Contents

Preface

In 1977, I was the treasurer of a small business investment company (SBIC) in metropolitan Washington, D.C. SBICs borrow large sums of money from the Small Business Administration and lend it to start-up companies or smaller businesses that need small amounts of cash for their business.

It wasn't exciting and, as you can imagine, working with the federal government meant completing reams of forms and submitting tons of reports. At that time, a client of the SBIC, a developer who knew I wanted to do something more creative, came to me and asked me if I wanted to do his public relations.

Until that time, most of my brief career had been spent in the advertising and promotion fields in New York. While I worked with public relations professionals during that time, I had not been involved in the details of the public relations aspect of business. I asked this developer exactly what he had in mind, and he said, "Well, I'd like you to get a 'squib' in *The Washington Post* and some articles in business publications about my company." Being very naïve at the time, I thought, "How difficult could that be?"

I resigned my position at the SBIC and began work for my first client. I was now in business. I was a public relations consultant.

The first thing I did was to buy a basic book on public relations and read it from cover to cover. I had a client who was depending on me to get him "squibs" in the *Post*, and I wanted to do everything right.

And, indeed, within six weeks, my client was mentioned in the real estate section of *The Washington Post*. Mission accomplished! But that was only the beginning. This client referred me to other small business owners and they became my clients.

One year later, I had a stable of clients who kept me busy all the time. One day I received a mailer from a major professional education organization offering a three-day course in New York City on basic public relations. I took the time off to take the course and when I completed it, I realized that I had been doing pretty much the right thing in my fledgling business.

I continued to read about public relations and to take more courses. I joined the Public Relations Society of America (PRSA)—the preeminent organization for this specialty. I met with my peers regularly. I became involved in the profession. Public relations became my passion.

In 1983, I took the grueling two-day exam to become accredited by PRSA. This designation puts public relations professionals who earn this degree in a special category that makes them stand out from the crowd of public relations practitioners. I passed the exam and earned my APR—"Accredited in Public Relations."

In 1987, I sold my public relations business and became the first full-time public relations director of the American Pharmaceutical Association (APhA). Pharmacists became a very special constituency for me, and I have devoted years to working with the media on their behalf.

When pharmacists would contact me and ask how they could work with their local media, I would send them information I had compiled that might be useful to their efforts. I also conducted media training courses for the APhA leadership when they came to town. Recently, after so many years of working with pharmacists to publicize their efforts, I thought it was time to put some of these ideas into a book especially for pharmacists.

I have designed this book to be used in whole or in part. For example, I have included detailed information on writing a news release and getting on television. These are basic outreach tactics. If done correctly, they pay dividends in good exposure. If you have a lot of experience with the media but just need to know a few specifics, you can go directly to that chapter for the information. If you are a novice and want to begin a modest public relations program, that, too, is available. If you want to hire a public relations company to handle your public relations, there are tips on how to select a public relations firm.

I have also included a chapter specifically for students. While students may find the entire book to be useful to them, they do have some special needs that I have attempted to address.

I hope you find this book helpful in conducting your public relations outreach efforts, but, more importantly, I hope you have fun while you're doing it!

Public Relations and Your Professional Image

Public sentiment is everything. With public sentiment, nothing can fail; without it, nothing can succeed.

—Abraham Lincoln, 1859

If you've opened this book, you're probably already interested in public relations. What you're looking for is some practical, down-to-earth guidance on how to make it happen.

At first, public relations may seem like a complicated and time-consuming task—a job for a journalist or media professional, not a healthcare professional like yourself. As a busy pharmacist, you may wonder how you can fit public relations into your other activities.

Public relations is indeed a profession, and you may even want to get the assistance of a public relations professional to help you develop and carry out your program. The major purpose of this book, however, is to convince you that you don't need a communications or public relations background to mount a modest but successful public relations campaign for your pharmacy practice. What you do need are certain basic tools, persistence, and the time to devote to selling your story to the media.

This book will give you the tools and the guidance you need to do just that. It focuses on the elements most applicable to helping pharmacists get their messages to their "publics"—the specific audiences with whom it is most important for pharmacists to communicate.

You will learn, one step at a time, exactly what you have to do to conduct a credible and successful public relations program—one that is tailored to your services and your public relations goals.

PR and Your Professional Image: The Need for Goodwill

In a competitive marketplace, the survival of any profession depends on the amount of goodwill that is established. For the pharmacist, absence of goodwill is costly in terms of lost patients and poor productivity and cooperation from your associates.

Goodwill is the good relationship of a business enterprise or profession with its publics. It is gained by

▶ offering quality services,

▶ treating patients fairly,

▶ extending good human relations in all dealings, and

▶ performing necessary services for the community.

All these activities, which seem like a normal, commonsense way of doing good business, are part of public relations.

Those of you who have operated successful practices for years need not be reminded of the value of human relations. People want friendly, personalized attention and will seek out the pharmacist who offers understanding and a sympathetic ear.

Goodwill is established by how patients are treated, by the services and information made available to them, and even by how their complaints are handled. These are critical to the patient's satisfaction with the profession. Such considerations are part of the full-scale public relations program.

What Is Public Relations?

Although the principles of public relations have been around for hundreds of years, the formal practice of the craft is less than 100 years old. Today, the term *public relations* is used so frequently, and misused as well, that there's a tendency to forget what the two words mean. The term is quite literal. It means relations—the way you meet, deal with, and are perceived by the public. Public relations is creating a climate in a community so that the goals and programs of your pharmacy practice are understood, accepted, and, it is hoped, supported.

Beyond the literal definition, public relations is the sum of a great many factors designed to give the public an impression about you and your pharmacy practice that is favorable, informed, and conducive to their doing more business with you. Basically, it's an attitude of courtesy, helpfulness, and professionalism.

Whenever anyone is involved in evaluating public attitudes, spelling out policies and procedures in the people's best interests, and earning public understanding and acceptance of their causes, they are practicing public relations.

Public Relations Encompasses Many Different Activities

- counseling
- research
- media relations
- publicity
- employee and member relations
- community relations
- public affairs
- government affairs
- issues management
- financial relations
- industry relations
- development and fundraising
- minority relations and multicultural affairs
- special events and public participation
- marketing communications

Publicity is part of public relations, but it is not synonymous with it. Public relations is an ongoing activity that should permeate every aspect of your practice. Publicity is a tool of public relations that deals with communication—with using the media to tell your story. Appendix A provides definitions of terms commonly used in the public relations field; knowing the difference between them can help you in your public relations efforts. Appendix B answers some "Frequently Asked Questions."

Public relations can be a major addition to promoting goods, services, products, or ideas. It can also show that there is more than one side to a controversial issue. It can turn an audience around on an issue, if you have the facts and use common sense. And it can help your pharmacy practice get its story across and possibly minimize damage done by outside forces.

One key element of public relations is disseminating the facts about your pharmacy practice in a way that makes you more visible and better known to your market. On this level, public relations uses a number of techniques, including publicity, designed to disseminate that information. It includes a number of activities, such as community events, that make your pharmacy practice better known and thought of more favorably. In this context, one popular definition of public relations applies—doing well by doing good.

Advertising Versus Publicity: What's the Difference?

The objectives of publicity are in many ways parallel to those of advertising; for example, both involve imparting information and enhancing reputation. However, there are several important distinctions between the two functions.

Because advertising is purchased, it enables you to be persuasive in your own words and in your own way. Publicity, on the other hand, depends upon a presumably objective third person—the editor—who is more concerned with meeting the needs of his or her publication than with meeting your need to inform.

If the editorial thrust of a publication is not consistently meeting the needs of its readers, it will lose circulation, diminish its value as an advertising medium, and go out of business. This reality is as true of the smallest community newspaper as it is of *The New York Times* or *The Chicago Tribune*. It's as true of the smallest and most remote radio station as it is of the largest network.

Thus, while advertising can be prepared to persuade the reader or listener directly, publicity must be structured to meet the editorial needs of a publication or the broadcast media. The person to be persuaded is the editor, not the reader. While advertising techniques are designed to bring the message directly to the reader, publicity techniques are designed to persuade the editor that the message fulfills the publication's editorial needs.

What Public Relations Can and Can't Do for You

Public relations can pay big dividends for you by getting your messages out to your target audiences and into the minds of the people who make important business decisions.

What's more, you can reap these dividends without a large financial investment. Although it is possible to spend thousands of dollars on a high-image public relations campaign, it's also possible, as you will see in the chapters that follow, to develop a great public relations program without spending much money at all. Public relations can achieve many of the same effects as advertising without costing you a fortune. Positive publicity is earned, while advertising is bought.

Public relations builds credibility. When your public relations efforts result in favorable publicity, you have the added advantage of the implied editorially objective report—the third-party endorsement of the publication or broadcast affiliate, which appears to be saying, objectively, that because you are newsworthy you are to be viewed favorably.

Now for the bad news. Although you can do a lot to increase the chances that the media will pick up your leads, there is no guarantee that they will. Moreover, their priorities may not be the same as yours. You may have to be willing to compromise a bit. In advertising, by contrast, you have far greater control over the message.

Another downside of publicity is that a negative story, whether it is true or false, will create a negative reaction in the eyes of the public. As part of your public relations strategy, you must be prepared to counter negative stories.

Finally, public relations cannot change bad into good; counteract a lack of integrity; substitute image for substance; or transform an undeserving service, cause, or organization into a highly regarded service, cause, or organization.

So what can public relations do for you? Basically, whatever you want it to do. The secret is knowing what to do with it.

Pharmacy's Publics

One of the first things you must think about as you move forward with a public relations campaign is how to define your publics. Every business and profession has publics. These are the various groups you serve whose opinions of you and your practice have a vital effect on your professional image and the image of your pharmacy.

The needs of each public are different, and the way in which you communicate with them will vary accordingly. Each must be handled with understanding and wisdom if you want to win and maintain public approval. Because your time and resources are limited, you should also decide where you want to focus the majority of your public relations efforts.

Success is a matter of being on the alert for opportunities to tell your message to your publics and to target it as closely as you can to their needs.

Who Are Pharmacy's Publics?

Your first, and most important, one is your patients. Pharmacy's publics also include physicians, dentists, nurses, associates, drug wholesalers, manufacturers and all other suppliers, and your professional colleagues.

The Media Need You

If you've never dealt with the media, it's important to recognize one thing: They need you as much as you need them. Good media relationships are a win–win situation. Both sides have a great deal to gain.

Some media stories—for example, a local crime, a devastating hurricane, or an international summit meeting—create themselves. The media cover the stories and follow through by investigating unique story angles or personal asides that enrich the coverage and make it more appealing.

But newspapers, magazines, radio, and television also rely extensively on information generated by individuals and businesses for the content of their news stories. The media use many sources to gather the lineup of stories that they cover. If your strategy works as you hope it will, those sources can include you!

For example, most feature stories in the major weekly news magazines are inspired by public relations efforts. Cover stories on society, cultural or intellectual trends, movies, entertainment or business personalities, breakthroughs in health or education, and even the weather, do not just happen. They are created by the media and public relations people working together.

This book focuses on situations in which you are either proactively working with the media on a local angle to a national news story or offering your expertise to the media as an expert analyst. Such proactive encounters with the media put your information into the hands of consumers.

To succeed in public relations, you must, therefore, reach out to the media. You might think of the media as one of the important channels through which you will communicate your message to your publics. Obtaining positive publicity—news, feature, or editorial coverage in newspapers and magazines, on radio and television—is a fundamental activity for a successful public relations program. Editorial statements made by the media influence the public because an independent third party is seen as making remarks about you and the profession of pharmacy.

Public Relations as an Ongoing Process

By now it should be clear that public relations is not something that you turn on and off at will. The public relations attitude that projects the concept of service is an ongoing and never-ending affair. It should be a constant in any profession.

But public relations is more than just an attitude of "niceness" or even of service. It must function in a realistic context of sound business practice and excellence. News of poor business techniques will travel farther and faster than you can possibly offset with even the most sophisticated publicity campaign. At the same time, the good things you do, the services you perform, and those activities that contribute to the very reputation you'd like to have also travel well.

Publicity, too, should be an ongoing affair, whether you do it yourself or use an outside agency. There should be a steady flow of news to your local media. You should become publicity minded, not in the sense of being egotistical or excessively bold, but in the professional sense of being a reliable source of health information for local media. It's a better idea to send out information regularly rather than to mount a media blitz once a year. If you issue a steady flow of information, your news sources will get to know you and your practice and will come to think of you as a reliable source of useful health information.

Plan on setting aside some time on a daily, weekly, or monthly basis to put your program into action. To make your program effective, you're going to have to make it a priority. Keep yourself visible among the media so that when they need an expert for a story they will call on you.

For many pharmacists, engaging in public relations and seeking publicity require a change of mind-set. It entails seeing what you are doing from a different perspective—that of your patient, of a community member, or even of a competitor—and trying to identify a "hook" that will draw their attention. It may be that your pharmacists have been trained in herbal products or your practice specializes in lipid monitoring. It may be a newsworthy event that you develop or sponsor and then report to the local media. Consistency is important to making you a valuable and interesting source of information for the local media and to garner more publicity for yourself, thereby increasing your visibility.

Public relations, in other words, is cumulative. For example, a news story may lead to an invitation to speak before a local citizens' group; this speech, in turn, may lead to an invitation to appear on TV or to join an influential committee. The results of public relations occur over the long term. The benefits may not be immediate, but they will inevitably appear.

No single marketing tactic can be counted on to miraculously bring in new business. But a number of marketing activities, when used to maximum effect, can help position your practice in a way that over the long term inevitably leads to an increase in business.

One type of public relations effort affects another. When you are quoted in the local newspaper, you can use that quotation to get quoted in a regional magazine or a national newspaper or to get speaking engagements. When you are invited to speak, you can invite members of the media to attend and you might get quoted in the newspaper or on radio.

Building a Public Relations Strategy

In public relations, like in any other field, you need a strategic plan. In this plan, you should set forth a well thought out and executable strategy to identify and reach out to the individual publics important to your pharmacy practice and to keep them informed of your goals and programs. You should also define what your message will be.

Tie your plan to the calendar. Outline what will be done in each step, and by when. A public relations effort occurs in stages. It includes preparation, inquiries with targeted organizations, and follow-up based on the priorities you have established. Establish a time line for your efforts.

PERSONAL EXAMPLE

The Long-Lived Clip

One pharmacist I know who has been aggressively pursuing public relations activities over the last five years says he is constantly amazed at how unpredictable are these effects. An article he wrote over a year earlier will generate a call from a reporter. He realizes now that individuals often clip things or make notes to themselves and put them aside until they feel they can use them.

You should also define your objectives in terms that you will be able to measure later on when you are evaluating the outcome of your program.

How can you set objectives? If you're starting out, be as focused as possible and don't be overly ambitious. As a pharmacist, you may be seeking to reach hospital administrators or healthcare executives. Getting quoted in *Golf Digest* probably won't do you a lot of good in reaching that audience.

You also need to determine the best means of reaching your audience. In other words, which media and organizations reach the targeted individuals most directly? Do you want to target national business media or local electronic media; trade journals or speaking engagements? Establish your top priorities and spell them out as clearly as possible. Identify them as precisely as possible, with names and individual contacts.

You must also determine your unique strengths. If you are a good speaker, you might want to focus on getting speaking engagements. If you are not a good speaker, however, you might focus more on writing articles or getting yourself quoted in newspapers. This is not to say that you should only engage in those activities in which you are strongest. Your goal should be a well-rounded effort, and this requires developing skills in a number of areas.

Think about organizational strengths as well. What are the areas in which your pharmacy really shines in comparison with the competition? What new services have you developed? Include those as key points in defining your message.

Set specific targets in terms of where you want to gain publicity and how frequently. How many articles do you want to have published and in which publications? On which radio and television programs do you want to appear? How many speeches do you want to give and to whom? Make sure your goals are realistic, with an eye toward the conservative. You typically won't get publicized in all the places you would like. By taking that into account, you won't create so wide a gap between goals and realities that you are discouraged from continuing.

Once you have answered these questions, you have begun to articulate a public relations strategy. And once you have put a written strategy together, you will be much more inclined to follow through and to determine what is possible.

Public Relations Do's

Be clear about your goals. Rather than writing dozens of news releases about all kinds of topics, choose the topics that your publics most need to know about and concentrate your efforts on these.

Know to whom you are talking. Take stock of your publics and work on each according to its importance. Know how to reach those publics. For instance, which radio station in your area is the best one to appear on to attract the age group you want to target?

Be able to measure what you do. Many public relations activities are intangible. Results are difficult to pinpoint. Other outcomes, however, are measurable if you take the time. How effective is a news release in publicizing an upcoming health screening? Does it increase the number of patients who come to your practice site? Improvements in a pharmacy newsletter can be measured by increased positive feedback from readers and a higher satisfaction rating in reader surveys.

Get to know the media that count and to know what they'll use. You'd be surprised at the number of people who send photos to radio station newsrooms or submit trade stories to national media outlets. It's a waste of money, to be sure. Perhaps even more importantly, if done repeatedly, it makes journalists feel you don't know what you're doing. They'll be unlikely to call you should an occasion arise when they need pharmacist input.

Build up a list of media contacts. This list will simplify the job of contacting them with your news releases. Program their numbers into your fax machine to make life easier, then spend the time saved in avoiding a mailing by phoning them as well. The personal sell can sometimes work where the piece of paper doesn't. E-mail is also an effective communications tool.

Enjoy—and be seen enjoying—what you do. Public relations is about presenting a positive image. If you don't believe in your project, who will?

Pharmacy's Messages

Pharmacists have important messages to communicate to the public and if you don't communicate these messages, you'll lose out on an important means of advancing your cause.

What Does the Profession Have to Say?

The box on the following page provides you with some messages that you may want to work into in your public relations campaign. Or you can develop your own themes that represent your practice or patients more specifically.

How Can You Get Your Messages Across?

How do you make sure that your message will be heard and understood? Think about it from the reader's or viewer's perspective. What do your patients want to know about a new therapy or service you are providing? Think about the questions they ask when they come to your practice site. Design your public relations message with a typical patient in mind.

Consider the following:

▶ Will your message be of interest to the general public? To determine whether a story you have in mind is likely to arouse interest, compare it with stories a magazine, newspaper, or radio station usually run.

Some Messages Pharmacists Need to Get Out

In the last quarter century, pharmacy has expanded its role within healthcare from a profession focusing on preparation and dispensing of medications to patients to one in which pharmacists provide a range of patient-oriented services to maximize the medicine's effectiveness.

Pharmacy is practiced in a wide range of settings: community pharmacies, chain pharmacies, hospitals, long-term-care facilities, the pharmaceutical industry, mail service, managed care, and government.

Medications have great power to heal and to improve the quality of life for millions of Americans; however, they may do serious harm if not taken correctly. This is where the role of the pharmacist is most important. Patients should choose their pharmacist carefully.

It is best to use only one pharmacy so that all medication records are at one location. In this way, there will be less risk of duplicating prescriptions or having one prescription interact harmfully with another.

Pharmacists who know their patients and have their medication profiles on file will be aware of possible harmful drug interactions and allergies to certain drugs. The pharmacist also will be able to discuss possible side effects; what foods, drinks, or activities the patient should avoid while taking a medication; what patients should do if they miss a dose; and a wide range of other helpful information.

The pharmacist is a key healthcare professional in helping people achieve the best results from their medications. Patients should choose a pharmacist they trust and build a partnership for good health.

As the leading healthcare authority on medication, the pharmacist is the most logical member of the healthcare team to gauge the usage and efficacy of medication, patients' medication use patterns, and alternative therapies.

Americans spend more than $100 billion per year on prescription and nonprescription drugs. Pharmacists as pharmaceutical care managers can help eliminate unnecessary costs by improving medicine use.

Health plans that provide coverage for physician and hospital services but do not adequately cover prescription drugs are shortsighted. Payment for diagnosis but not for treatment is a misuse of our limited financial resources.

▶ Is the story timely? Look for an element that makes the story timely—why the story should be run this week, rather than next week or last week.

▶ Why do you want coverage? To attract patients? Overcome a negative image?

▶ Whom are you trying to reach? The over-60's, teenagers, young mothers? The target group will determine what media to approach and what your message should be.

Maximizing the Impact of Good Publicity

As your public relations program matures, your publicity will go to work for you. One good story or interview will lead to another.

One of the best things about public relations is that it can be self-perpetuating. No single article or event is decisive; what's important is the snowballing effect. When a publicity mention appears in a publication, its audience is limited. The number of people who might ultimately see the item, benefit from it, and act on it, however, is vastly greater. For that reason, anyone taking public relations seriously should do everything possible to make that publicity work—over and over again. That requires keeping track of how and when a given item was used and making every effort to ensure that someone who might have missed the original article or TV segment still gets a chance to see it.

Any publicity you get should become a regular part of the media information you send out. Clippings can also be reproduced as part of a printed mailing piece and distributed to a select audience.

Many magazines will sell you reprints of the stories that have been published about you. Other publications will lend you the color separations and copy and allow you to have reprints made by your own printer. Reprints must be ordered early, usually when the magazine is being printed. When your story is accepted for publication, ask the editor how you can order reprints.

You may subscribe to a clipping service (see list on page 15). You may also prepare your own clippings. When doing so, make sure that you clearly indicate on each clipping the name and date of the publication and the number of the page on which it appeared. If you were featured in a color publication, especially if it has photos, invest in color photocopies. They are much more impressive than black-and-white copies. The nicer your clips look, the more likely they will be read.

With permission, you may also republish your news articles on the Web, but be sure to ask permission first. Some journalists may help you obtain permission from their publishers. It never hurts to ask.

Finally, don't forget to make sure that your internal audiences see the clips. Be sure your own staff is aware of any publicity you have received. Bulletin

PERSONAL EXAMPLE

Don't Believe Your Own Publicity

One of my former clients owned a multioffice real estate firm in Washington, D.C. After creating a public relations program that began with a local blitz, we decided that we would attempt to get some national coverage for her. I submitted a story about her to a national woman's magazine, suggesting that she be named one of the "Top 10 Women Entrepreneurs" of the year.

The magazine accepted our nomination and featured her in the article. When the story appeared, it was a major coup for the realtor. Her phone began ringing off the hook, with congratulations from the local community as well as from business people around the country. I began booking her on local radio and TV talk shows, and articles about her appeared in local newspapers and business magazines.

A few months later, at a Chamber of Commerce meeting, I received feedback about my client. She was not returning business phone calls, she was missing appointments, and she was being rude to her colleagues and business associates.

At one of my weekly meetings with the client, I mentioned the negative feedback that I had heard. I told her that it was canceling all of the good public relations efforts we had worked so hard on for the past year. She became arrogant, and I later resigned the account.

About six months later, I saw her at a business luncheon, and she confided to me that her business was suffering. I asked why she thought that was occurring and she said that she made the mistake of believing her own publicity! She thought she was more important than she was, and this had a negative effect on her relationships with her clients and business associates. It was a difficult, painful, and financially devastating lesson learned.

Keep a level head, stay humble, and don't believe your own publicity!

boards and company publications are ideal vehicles for displaying news items about the pharmacy practice to employees.

A neatly bound scrapbook of the pharmacy's clippings provides a casual, yet impressive, way to convey the stature of your pharmacy to your patients in your waiting area. Clippings can also be enlarged and used as backdrops in your window displays. If you have a Web site, be sure to keep it current with your latest clippings and news.

Evaluating the Outcome of Your Public Relations Efforts

How do you tell whether your efforts to create good public relations are paying off? It's not always easy to measure goodwill. However, the more targeted your campaign, the easier it will be to evaluate it.

Make Your Objectives Measurable

There are a number of ways to measure the success of a public relations campaign. To do so, you must first set measurable objectives. If your goal is media outreach, for example, you should identify the primary media for each effort and direct most of your attention to them.

Then find out how frequently your story idea was used and, equally important, whether the media pickup included the points that you consider important. Were your stories well used? Were you able to get relatively good position in the publication? Was your practice site mentioned? Was a photo used?

When evaluating how the media have used your material, don't overlook timing. You'll naturally be less satisfied if the media used a video clip at 2:00 a.m. than at 6 p.m.

In short, success cannot be measured in clip "tonnage" but rather on the basis of whether your material reached the targeted audience through the right media and whether the media did or did not bury it or cut it so much that the prime messages were lost. This will not, of course, measure whether the audience learned from it, but it will indicate that media objectives were met—and that is half the battle.

You will naturally want to focus on the media outlets that you have identified as most important to the publics you want to reach. Unless the messages are delivered in media that reach your primary audiences, you have not had a successful program. But you should not ignore the media that you have identified as secondary outlets. If an editor who is not especially important to your immediate needs contacts you for information, you are not obligated to help. But if you don't, it may have an adverse effect on your long-term media relations. You may need that editor's publication one day, the publication may be important to a colleague, or word may get around that you are uncooperative. Remember, too, that reporters and editors move around from one media outlet to another and they may wind up at one of your primary outlets down the road.

Finally, make sure that your expectations are reasonable. An appearance on the *Today* show or a story in *Newsweek* may be ego building, but it may not be the most effective way to reach your target audiences. Similarly, an exclusive story in a leading trade publication—following two in that same publication last year—may not be possible.

News Clipping and Other Services

How do you find out what the media are saying about your practice, your competitors, and your special interests? One way is to monitor publications yourself. Another is to have an assistant do it. A third way is to subscribe to a news clipping service.

When organizations need to monitor their own or a competitor's media coverage or to do subject research for a public relations campaign or a presentation, they often use a clipping service. These companies read the country's major daily and weekly newspapers, magazines, and trade publications and monitor the wire services, radio, and network and cable television news broadcasts. Clipping services clip all articles or transcribe or tape every broadcast that mentions any subject requested by their client company. Clips may be received on a daily or weekly basis. Organizations may find them useful when they need to know the exact words written or spoken by public figures for research, an organization briefing, news release, daily news update, or public relations campaign.

A major consideration in deciding whether to use a clipping service is the ultimate use of the clips. There are those who receive clips, admire them, show them to a few associates, and stuff them into a drawer where they may remain for years. Doing this is fine, but it does not take full advantage of your publicity. Press clippings have all sorts of strategic uses, including perpetuating the initial appearance of the item or article in a newspaper or magazine.

Most clipping services offer a range of services, including day-of-publication delivery, historical research, news clip analysis or public relations performance, and advertising analysis of competitors.

There are also services that monitor television and radio programming. Most major metropolitan areas have them. Check with a public relations firm in your area to see which services they would recommend.

These services are not inexpensive. Be prepared to spend about $150 for a videotape. On the plus side, the quality of the tape is good and the service can edit the tape to include the promos leading up to your segment.

Some Major Clipping Services

▶ **Allen's Press Clipping Bureau**
P.O. Box 2761
Los Angeles, CA 90051
(213) 628-4214

▶ **Bacon's Information**
332 S. Michigan Avenue
Chicago, IL 60604
(312) 922-2400

▶ **Burrelle's Information Services**
75 East Northfield Road
Livingston, NJ 07039
(973) 992-6600

▶ **Luce Press Clippings**
420 Lexington Avenue
New York, NY 10170
(212) 889-6711

Summary

Public relations is your total approach to the way you meet, deal with, and are perceived by everybody you want to do business with. It is a function of doing things well and making the things you do widely known so that people will want to do more business with you.

Public relations enhances your selling effort but rarely sells. It is apparent everywhere—in the way you conduct your practice, the way your practice site, your letterhead, and your Web site look, the way you answer a phone. It is a service-oriented attitude.

How will public relations help your practice grow and prosper? It will help you gain name recognition in a competitive marketplace; it will get your name out in front of your competitors; it will help you and your practice gain visibility in the community in which you live and work; and it will bring patients to your practice site.▶

CHAPTER 2

What the Media Want

The previous chapter discussed how public relations can enhance your professional image. It also presented some key considerations you will need to take into account when developing a public relations strategy.

This chapter focuses on the media—specifically, radio, television, newspapers, magazines, and journals—that you'll need to communicate your message to your various publics. It stresses how to identify the most appropriate media outlets for the message you have to convey, how to develop your message, and how to cooperate with editors and reporters to create a mutually beneficial relationship.

What Is News?

Healthcare is a competitive arena, and those involved in the field recognize the value of publicity in attracting patients as well as business. Pharmaceutical companies, which formerly promoted their products only to physicians and pharmacists, now arrange media tours for researchers. Hospitals, pharmacy schools, and voluntary health organizations issue news releases and hold media briefings. Scientific journals send out "tip sheets" or news releases to reporters, and it is not uncommon for these stories to make front-page news.

It has been said that news is what people are talking about. A nice simplification, but you need to know more. First, all news is relative. Each day, editors review all reported events and make subjective judgments as to which of those events will concern or interest their readers sufficiently to merit the allocation of space. On any given day, the news of a major airplane disaster will garner more editorial interest than a story about a major urban redevelopment plan. The urban plan, in turn, may preempt an announcement of a proposal to build a hospital in the community. And this, in turn, may preempt the news of plans to build a 50-room long-term-care facility. Still lower on the list would be an announcement of the appointment of a pharmacist as the president of the local Chamber of Commerce.

Because news is relative, you can never predict if your story will make the cut on a given day. If you're fortunate, it may be a slow news day, but it's always a matter that is completely beyond your control.

Where Does Your Public Relations Effort Begin?

Even though healthcare is one of the hottest topics covered by the media these days, pharmacy does not always factor into the media's coverage. Reporters and editors are constantly covering the pharmaceutical industry and physicians but many times overlook the contributions of the pharmacist, who is an integral part of the healthcare system. In the minds of some reporters and consumers, the pharmacist is secondary to the medications—simply a dispenser. They may be oblivious to the fact that pharmacists play a role in the delivery of healthcare to almost every American.

PERSONAL EXAMPLE

Don't Dare Compete with the Super Bowl

A former client wanted to schedule a news conference in Washington, D.C., to make an important announcement. He wanted to hold it on a Friday in January —a date that happened to be two days before the Super Bowl. This was not just any Super Bowl but one in which the Washington Redskins were playing. He also wanted to hold it on Capitol Hill because the message had political implications.

I tried to explain to my client the disadvantages of holding a news conference on that day, but he insisted on going through with it.

The big day came. Only two media outlets showed up. Of course, two people were better than none, but the poor attendance did not justify the amount of effort and resources that we spent on preparations for the news conference. On that particular day, what turned out to be news to the Washington press corps was having the local team as a contender in a major sporting event.

If you schedule an event, even if it's not just before Super Bowl Sunday, remember that there may be something else that will take the media's attention away from what you have spent weeks planning.

Americans take for granted the services provided by the pharmacist, because they have always received the advice and care of their pharmacist, unlike that of their physician, without an appointment or a bill. Every pharmacist has to help change that perception. The media can be an important ally in pharmacists' public relations efforts.

For starters, read the publications that you would like to see cover your issues, watch and listen to news broadcasts, and become familiar with the reporters covering healthcare. After doing this, you will easily be able to develop a list of media targets.

Cut down the job to size. If you have only one day a month to work on your public relations program, set your sights for a small-scale result. If your stories are local, concentrate only on local media. If your story warrants regional or national coverage, be prepared to give your campaign quite a bit more time.

The Focus of the Media

There are two basic media types: print and broadcast. Print media comprise newspapers (both daily and weekly) and periodicals (newsletters and magazines). Broadcast media include radio and television. Each medium has unique strengths and weaknesses that should be considered when targeting a message. Most major media outlets now also have Web sites. This gives them an added advantage of running stories almost as they occur. The use of Web sites serves to create very short deadlines.

The print media, for example, are able to provide in-depth commentary because they can publish long articles. They are not constrained to run short sound "bites." Another advantage of newspapers and magazines is that they have longer shelf lives than radio and TV.

News editors may occasionally consider health news of sufficient interest to their readers to be put in the general news section. Other newspapers make no distinction between news stories by industry, and a health story will have to compete for space with a school budget story. Increasingly, a health story is considered to be business news and falls under the business editor's domain.

A major city newspaper may have a separate staff for international news, another for national domestic news, and another just to cover the activities of the federal government. Other departments might include city news, business and finance, real estate, sports, art, theater, women's interests, and food. Some publications are large enough to be departmentalized, so that health news becomes the province of the health editor.

Even in the smallest newspapers, news is categorized, with an editor assigned to each category. A small community newspaper, with a staff of only three or four people, will categorize news by special interest, such as citywide news that affects the community, school news, health news, or sports.

In addition, every segment of the media has its own target audiences and therefore its own point of view. The big-city newspaper usually focuses on

Media Checklist

TV

▶ Television stations have local news programs, editorial opinions and "talk back" opportunities, public affairs programs, one-on-one interview shows, and public affairs specials.

▶ Community cable stations offer local news programming, community access channels, and public affairs programming.

▶ Public television stations provide local news programming as well as a diverse mix of locally produced public affairs programming.

Radio

▶ Radio formats include all-news stations, talk shows, public affairs programming, and editorial comment.

Newspapers

▶ Newspapers have numerous "beat" reporters covering specialized issues for the main news, editorial page, op-ed section, letters to the editor, the business section, consumer issues, and soft news.

international and national news. Local or regional news is relegated to a secondary position, except for matters of citywide significance. The community newspaper focuses entirely on local issues and people.

A major advantage of radio over the other media is immediacy. Radio, more than any other medium, is for breaking news. When speed counts, radio has the advantage of being able to produce and air a broadcast report minutes after news breaks. Radio also can have a more leisurely appeal. Morning drive time shows and evening rush hour programs often have large followings and loyal listeners—just as loyal as those who subscribe to a newspaper or magazine.

Television's strength is the ability to blend pictures with storytelling to create a compelling visual story that can leave a strong impression. Even television news is targeted to a defined audience. Some stations position their newscasts to reach a mass audience that's more interested in sensationalism than in politics. Others focus more heavily on government and national news.

Despite their differences, newspapers, magazines, radio, and TV have one thing in common: they have limited space or time. Editors must make fast decisions about their priorities. Any information that you have and believe to be newsworthy must compete against all the other news about which the editor must make a judgment for the next edition. By using appropriate publicity techniques, you can compete successfully for the editor's attention and win a judgment in your favor in the competition for space and time.

Evaluating News Appeal

But what determines whether a story is newsworthy? The essential elements of news value are

 ▶ timeliness,

 ▶ local appeal, and

 ▶ interesting subject matter.

Timeliness, of course, is key. Nothing beats breaking news. Such news stories often command front-page attention at newspapers and lead airtime at radio and TV stations. Breaking news is immediate news about something that just happened and that matters to a defined audience. This is news that people will talk about.

Most media are also extremely interested in stories with a local angle. Even if a story is a national story, you may be able to find a local angle in it that would interest the media in your area.

Conflict, whether it involves people, companies, or government, makes news. What may seem to be a simple rivalry between two business competitors is often a good news story for the media. Don't be fooled by those who say they don't read negative stories—they do, and news editors know it.

Some people are newsworthy simply because of their fame or their position of power. People are interested in people. It's a fact and a strong element of news. Those who read, listen to, and watch the news like to learn about others. Playing up personal elements in your story will make it more interesting to viewers and readers.

How Newsworthy Is Your Story?

In evaluating the news appeal of a story, ask yourself these questions:

 ▶ What is the significance of your services or event to the general public?

 ▶ When a major health news story breaks, can it be related to your pharmacy or to the profession in general? Do you have expertise in the subject? For example, if new research on asthma treatment is publicized, does your pharmacy specialize in counseling or in providing additional services for the asthma patient?

 ▶ How does your expertise, special event, or unique service help the community?

 ▶ Are trends in society reflected in your pharmacy? For example, have you started providing a new level of pharmaceutical care, such as immunizations or hyperlipidemia monitoring? Do you have an interactive Web site? Do your print materials include your Web site address? Do you feature information on new drugs on your Web site?

Types of News

Several news categories offer publicity opportunities for pharmacists.

Straight News

In the course of your daily activities, any number of things might happen that are sufficiently out of the ordinary to warrant media attention.

If, for example, you've just introduced an innovative practice that specializes in disease state management and pharmaceutical care, it might well be news for the local paper and radio and TV stations. If you have formed a partnership with your local public health department to provide immunizations to school children, that, too, might be newsworthy. If your pharmacy is involved in a demonstration project on monitoring drug therapy that is part of a national study, it might well be considered newsworthy by local media.

Depending upon the size of your practice and the size of the community in which it functions, some personnel news may be newsworthy as well. By monitoring the local media carefully—the media that serve your market area—you can get a fair idea of the kinds of activities and events that might warrant publication or airtime.

Feature Stories

Newspapers do not run on news alone. They have an entertainment as well as an educational function. The amusing human interest story or the article on how to get the most from a pharmacist is as important to a newspaper as a front-page story.

Developing feature materials is a significant part of publicity. As a pharmacist, you're in a good position to use your expertise to develop these features. And since a pharmacist deals with people and people do amusing things, you can be a prime source of interesting stories.

Invited Articles

Magazines, Sunday supplements, and some newspapers are delighted to consider articles written by outside authors, provided they have an accurate, appealing story to tell. Local media are constantly looking for information to help their readers be better consumers. Such topics would include articles on how to take their medicine correctly, how to stock their medicine cabinet, and what the instructions on their prescriptions really mean. The possibilities are endless. One major advantage of writing your own article is that you have greater control over the content (subject to the editor's input).

"Manufacturing" News Events

You can do many things to create a newsworthy event. Typical examples are the kinds of events discussed in Chapter 7, such as workshops, screenings, and clinics for the public, as well as community health promotion programs. Pharmacists, like chefs and caterers (see page 23), can create news opportunities. You may want to approach your local television or radio station and offer to be a regular guest health expert on one of their programs or on the local news. Be prepared with several different topics that you could discuss. Don't be afraid to think "outside the box." You may actually be able to overcome an obstacle that the producer is facing but doesn't have the resources to solve. This is where having a relationship with the producer can pay off. Rather than just say the station can't do a health segment, the producer may share with you why she thinks they can't do it. This gives you an opportunity to come up with a solution and move everyone's agenda forward.

Other types of news opportunities that might work include health screenings. For example, hold a diabetes screening at your pharmacy and invite the mayor and other local celebrities. Let the media know you will be conducting this event and see if they can cover it.

If you want to create opportunities, let your imagination be your guide. And don't let challenges get in your way.

Media Lists

A media list is a compilation of the potential outlets for the stories that you wish to share. It should include as much information as you need to get your message to the right person at the outlet—name, title, phone number, fax number, and e-mail address, for example. Your list should include both print and broadcast media. Use it to pitch stories to the media, invite the media to events, mail reports, and send news releases.

Make sure that all major media outlets in your area are on your list. However, it is also important to pay attention to smaller outlets, such as ethnic publications and college radio stations. Don't forget radio and TV talk shows. The more outlets you target, the better your chance for coverage. Think broadly.

Preparing Your Media List

Many sources will aid you as you prepare media lists. Reading the newspaper, watching television, and talking with other professionals who work on the issues you care about are good ways to find out who should be included on your list. Many news outlets have Web sites that give you access to their publications and staff, and some allow you to e-mail reporters directly. Sometimes local organizations, the Chamber of Commerce, or the convention bureau have developed a media directory. You can find out if your area has one by calling a local public relations firm and asking the firm to recommend one.

PERSONAL EXAMPLE

Creating a Demand for Bunnies and Turkeys

One of my former clients, a caterer, was one of the few candy manufacturers in Washington, D.C. For Easter, the company made hundreds of pounds of chocolate bunnies and eggs filled with candy. I decided to send a huge chocolate egg filled with Easter treats to Willard Scott at NBC in New York.

Willard opened the egg in front of the viewing audience and shared the delicious contents with his cohosts. He mentioned my client and thanked him for this beautiful and tasty treat.

During the next few weeks, orders for these eggs came flooding into my client from all over the country. I'm not sure he was prepared for the response, but he did fill all the orders.

In my public relations business, I also represented several Washington restaurants. For Thanksgiving one year, I persuaded one of my clients to invite a local TV reporter to a Thanksgiving dinner at his restaurant the week before the holiday. We staged a Thanksgiving dinner for about 12 people in a private room at the restaurant.

The table looked spectacular. There was a beautiful floral centerpiece, candelabra, roasted turkey with all the trimmings, and several different pies for dessert. The reporter and his crew were astonished at the spread. The entire dinner was filmed as a family affair with the reporter joining as one of the guests. It was run as a short human interest segment on the television affiliate a few days before Thanksgiving.

Reservations at the restaurant peaked. Those who couldn't get a reservation ordered a turkey dinner from the restaurant to take home. We had created a spectacular event, and we all got to enjoy the delicious food.

This same client asked me if I could get him a regular guest spot on one of

Continued on the next page.

Media Directories

You may use a media directory to help you compile your list. Here are some media directories you may find at your local library:

- *The Gebbie Press, All-In-One Directory.* Includes all media—radio, TV, newspapers, magazines, black and Hispanic media, networks, Associated Press/United Press International bureaus, and news syndicates.
- *Bacon's.* A four-volume set covering newspapers, magazines, radio, and TV.
- *Broadcasting & Cable Yearbook.* A single volume covering radio and TV.
- *Working Press of the Nation.* A three-volume set covering newspapers, magazines, radio, and TV.
- *Burrelle's.* A three-volume set that includes newspapers, magazines, radio, and TV.
- *Editor & Publisher Year Book.* Lists daily and weekly newspapers.
- *Gale Research.* A three-volume set covering publications, broadcast media, and newspapers.

PERSONAL EXAMPLE *continued*

the local Washington television affiliate's morning shows for a cooking segment. Since I had worked with the producer many times, I approached her with this opportunity. She said that it sounded like a great idea to have a regular cooking segment on the show; however, she expressed concern about the logistics in preparing hot food on the set.

I went back to my client, and we discussed this challenge. He offered to have a cooking surface built that he would donate to the television station. It would include an electric stovetop and heating ovens built into a table that was on casters for ease and mobility. In exchange, I asked that he be a regular guest on that cooking segment twice a month. The cooking segment would be featured five days a week. Having this "prop" allowed the producer to invite other guest chefs on the show to participate in the new cooking segment.

The producer accepted our offer. Eventually, some of my other clients were also featured guests on this show—all because the problem of how to cook on the television set was solved. It was a win for all involved.

Script for Gathering Media Contact Information

Hello. My name is Kathy Jones with Arcade Pharmacy, and I'm in the process of updating our media list. Will you please tell me the name, title, phone number, e-mail address, and fax number of the person who covers healthcare issues at your organization?

Thank you for your time.

Note: Be sure to ask for the correct spelling of all names.

Importance of Accuracy

Whether you order a national directory, use a local one, or compile your own list from firsthand sources, check all contact names before sending information or making a call to pitch a story. Editors and reporters change beats frequently, and a news release sent to the wrong reporter usually ends up in the trash.

To get the information you need, simply call the media outlet and ask who is covering your issue area. For pharmacy, the typical issue area is health, but your specific issue could apply to the metro or business section. You don't necessarily need to speak with each reporter. If the outlet has a receptionist, let him or her know that you are updating or preparing a media list and would like information regarding some specific contacts. Pharmacy interns can be useful in doing this work, but be sure they understand the need for accuracy.

Using a Media List

In most cases, you will not need to use your entire list. Depending upon the nature of the event you are holding or the information you are releasing, you may only need a part of it. For each event or release, target the type of outlet that is most suitable for your story. Most stories are suitable for print and radio. If your story is visual (e.g., you will be holding a media briefing about Medicare in front of a nursing home), target television as well.

While it is important to develop rapport with reporters and editors, be careful not to overuse your media list. Call or send materials to reporters or editors only for those specific issues and events that you know will appeal to them.

Update your lists regularly to ensure that the information you disseminate reaches the intended contacts. Media outlets often have high turnover rates, and the health reporter you contacted for your last release may no longer be employed at that outlet or may work a different beat. Call each contact or outlet before sending a major news release or conducting an event to ensure you are reaching the appropriate person.

If a story develops from your initial query, you may find yourself working with someone whose name is not on the list. Make sure that new names are added and names that are no longer valid are regularly deleted.

Communicating with the Media

Now that you've created your media list, you are ready to communicate with the media. You may communicate indirectly through a print, audio, or video medium or directly via telephone, news conference, or, less commonly, personal visit.

How do the media like to get information from you? Just ask them. Preferences vary. The bureau chief of a major wire service in Washington, D.C., for example, will not look at anything unless he receives it by e-mail. Others prefer a fax. As quickly as technology is moving, electronic transmission of news releases may soon become the preferred way of sending and receiving information.

The basic tool supplied to journalists is a news release (see Chapter 4). Other materials that may be of interest to the media include copies of speeches and statements, news clips, reports, film clips, audiotapes, and video news releases. The telephone is the most frequently used tool of direct access for reporters to live sources. Others include news conferences, media briefings (a less formal version of the news conference), speeches, demonstrations, and teleconferences.

Building a Relationship with Reporters and Editors

It is essential to know the media and the representatives who write about or comment on your practice or your issues. Their buy-in will determine in large part whether your public relations program is successful. Developing a productive relationship with reporters and editors doesn't require that you be golf buddies, lunch partners, or fraternity brothers or sorority sisters. But you do need to know who they are, and they should know who you are and what interests you represent.

Trust and How to Earn It

A successful relationship is based on trust, and trust must be earned. Once it is, editors will come to respect your judgment. The material you send or the ideas you present will be seen as news, your feature ideas will be listened to, and invitations to your media event will be taken seriously. Maintaining a professional relationship may make a difference in the frequency and extent of coverage of your practice.

Many editors base their decision about whether to use a news release on the reputation of the organization and the source. It is beneficial, therefore, when the editor spots the name of the organization contact and recognizes someone who is known and respected and has a reputation for submitting material that is pertinent to the reader. But there's another side too. If the material is consistently of little value, you may get a bad reputation, and whatever you send will be regarded with suspicion or ignored.

Journalists will respect you and your cause if you are courteous and professional with them. If a reporter has covered your issue in a favorable way, call and thank him or her for the coverage. You should also call reporters if they've reported inaccuracies—but be polite about it. Call journalists you know with tips about issues other than yours that you think might interest them. Don't ever call a reporter close to deadline, and always ask them if they're on deadline. It's good to start a conversation by first identifying yourself and your affiliation and asking a reporter, "Do you have a minute?"

If you are unable, for whatever reason, to answer a question, explain your position by saying, for example, "I'm not in a position to answer that question now because...". The reporter may not agree with your stance, but he or she won't feel you are stonewalling if you explain why you cannot answer. Mutual respect will be maintained if you have done your job in developing good relations.

A Two-Way Street

Members of the media are people first and reporters second. If things click between you and a reporter, do what you can to further the relationship. You may want to invite him or her to lunch or for coffee or to simply stay in touch regularly.

Why is this important? Though the reporter may not be able to do another story for you for a while, he or she may know of other reporters who are working on related pieces. The reporter can also provide invaluable advice on getting in touch with other media representatives.

Working with the media is a two-way street. You may be able to do favors for them, too. Perhaps they need suggestions about a news story they are working on, and you may know people to recommend they talk to or have ideas as to where they can go for more information on the subject.

Get to know reporters and editors in your area. Call them even before you have a story idea, introduce yourself, and find out about them. What are their deadlines? What is their beat? How can you be helpful to them when they are covering health stories? You might try scheduling an introductory visit with editors to acquaint them with your activities and issues that affect the community. For example, they may not be aware that a large employer in your community has restricted its employees' prescription drug benefits to a closed network of pharmacies, affecting citizens' access to and quality of care. If you establish yourself as a valid source for news, they may turn to you in the future for help with a story.

Ultimately, you'll want to establish a personal relationship with as many editors as possible. If an editor thinks that you have a large enough story or, more important, that you might be a consistent source of news, he or she will be delighted to accept an invitation from you for lunch. Most editors are professionals and build personal relationships slowly. They are not swayed by gifts or elaborate presentations; just the story will do. Then you're doing your job and they're doing theirs.

Regardless of how you make your initial contact, you must do your homework. This means being prepared to describe your story idea clearly and succinctly and to answer the listener's questions.

Does a personal relationship with an editor make a difference? Only in that you're more likely to get a hearing for a story you have for the editor's publication. Few editors allow a personal relationship to affect their judgment of what's acceptable for their publication, nor are the friendliest editors likely to print a story as a favor to you that's not consistent with the editorial needs of their publication. To ask a journalist to give you valuable space because of friendship rather than the quality of the news is to take unfair advantage of the friendship and jeopardize the journalist's position with the publication.

Using the Phone

At times, you may want to phone a reporter, editor, or producer directly to see if he or she is interested in a certain subject before sending out your material. This step would be especially appropriate if your material might become out of date quickly. That way, if one reporter is not interested in the subject, you can contact someone else at the same publication or program.

Your story may be a business story, in which case you'll want the business editor. Or it might be the kind of story that should go to an appropriate features editor. The simplest way to find the right editor is to call the publication and ask for the name of the editor who covers the kind of story you have.

When you phone, be sure you know exactly what you want to say. Many reporters and editors answer their own phones, so do not be surprised if you get through to them instantly. This makes it doubly important that you be prepared. Make notes beforehand if necessary so that you can quickly get to the point.

Introduce yourself, explain that you have a story, tell the gist of the story in as few words as possible, and ask to see the editor. He or she will tell you very quickly whether the story is of any interest and whether it warrants further discussion. It may be a news item the editor can take over the phone. If it isn't a timely story that will be stale news within 24 hours, the editor might ask you to send it in writing. In that case, deliver it by hand, trusting the mail only for stories that will be as newsworthy a week from now as they are today. If the editor is interested in the story, you may be asked to come down to the publication and discuss it. If it's big news, the editor may assign someone to come to the site of the story to cover it.

Approaching a Reporter

TOP TIPS

Know the decision makers. Knowing whom to contact is half the news battle. Your time and the time of your staff are too valuable to be chasing down the wrong editor at the wrong address. Take a few minutes and glance through the media directories that can be found in your local library. These references provide you with the names, addresses, and phone numbers of health editors, reporters, and assignment editors.

Know your story. Get it clear in your mind, and check the publication to be sure that your format for presenting the story on paper is consistent with the publication's own techniques for reporting similar stories.

Choose the medium. Not every story is right for every publication. Know your media so that you can determine what story is right for what publication.

Find the right editor. In a small community weekly, it's easy—there's usually only one editor. At a large newspaper, there are many editors covering different departments. If your local papers have health editors, make it a point to know who they are and to meet them and let them know you. This process is best begun by having a story for them on the first contact.

Respect deadlines. A missed deadline means no news. Remember that pharmacy is not the only profession with daily deadlines and time constraints. Always respect a reporter's deadline. It is best to contact the media during the morning and early afternoon. A call on a Monday or Tuesday is also usually better received than one later in the week. If a reporter requests information or an interview and requests it quickly, grant the request promptly. Reporters are like elephants—they will remember that you helped them out; they will also remember if you do not.

Be persistent. Don't be discouraged if your local media do not run a story the first time that you approach them. Be assertive in suggesting interview and photo opportunities for the future. If a local radio station only has time to run a short announcement on your involvement in a newsworthy event, suggest your availability for an in-studio interview at a later date. If the health reporter at your community newspaper tells you a feature-length pharmacy story is in the works for a later time, invite that reporter to your practice for a day of observation.

Rules of Engagement

By adhering to the following guidelines, you can help ensure that you make a favorable impression on the media:

▶ Evaluate your media material beforehand. Is it worthy of their attention? Does it explain why your story is right for their medium?

▶ Respect their time. They will be grateful.

▶ Take reporters at their word. If a reporter or producer asks you to call back at a certain time, they mean it. Call back at the appointed hour. If they ask you to send them more information, do so that day.

▶ If you are speaking to them on the phone or in person, do not press your cause too hard. Present the positive aspects of your idea and then let the material you are giving them do the rest of the selling for you.

▶ Columnists usually want exclusivity on a story, so if you want a particular story done by a particular columnist send your material to that writer only and note that the material is being offered to him or her exclusively. Do not send information on the same subject to another person at each program or publication until you have a rejection from the person who received it first.

Steps to Contact the Media

▶ Decide on the message.

▶ Select the medium or media to be approached.

▶ Prepare or select proper written material.

▶ Find out to whom the material should be sent.

▶ Determine proper timing if necessary.

▶ Send the material.

▶ Follow up with a phone call if appropriate.

▶ Send a thank you note for publicity received.

▶ In a few days, follow up with a phone call. You may send out the material to the rest of the media after the columnist's piece has appeared. If the columnist is not going to use the material, you may offer it as an exclusive to someone else or send it out for general release.

▶ Provide background materials. If a member of the media invites you to come in for an interview or makes an appointment to come to you to do a story, be prepared to make the person's job as easy as possible. Any written material you can provide will be appreciated. If the media representative asks for anything more, try to send it as soon as you can.

If your story appears in print or an interview runs on radio or television, a thank you note is very much in order. That sort of thoughtfulness is a first step to becoming someone the media representative will remember and will want to work with again.

Expect the Unexpected

There is no way to guarantee the outcome of an interview with the media. Reporters and editors make the final decisions about how your material is used and what is to be said. If you're dealing with radio or TV, you cannot even control the time when your story will run. Even if a producer tells you that your story will appear on a specific day at a specific time, situations could arise that could affect that schedule. This is totally different from advertising, where you pay for the space and can control everything from the message to the day and the time it is run.

Summary

You can never be 100% sure that a story will air until it actually does. While it's reassuring to know that a segment will run—sometime—the uncertainty makes it difficult to secure local publicity and build a wide audience for the segment.

The media are always dealing with deadlines. They are constantly pushing and pulling to make things happen within their time schedule. Remember that every story is subject to being bumped by something the media consider more important or more timely, or even by programming changes. Chances are that your story will be aired eventually. You just have to be patient and play by the media's rules. ▶

Preempted Again!

I received a call from *CBS Evening News* on a Thursday afternoon before a Friday holiday. They were working on a story for a Sunday night news segment and wanted to interview a pharmacist about medication errors.

I identified an appropriate spokesperson and arranged for the taping on the Friday holiday. Unfortunately, the segment did not run that Sunday. It was preempted by a sporting event and rescheduled for the following Sunday. The network then fed the piece to its affiliates for broadcast on the Monday after it aired on the network. It subsequently aired on 19 affiliates in addition to the network.

How to Work with the Media

Chapter 2 focused on what the media want and how you can tailor your approach to the needs of print and broadcast outlets. This chapter explores these media outlets in greater detail. It begins by presenting details about newspapers, which remain one of the most widely used means of communication. It then discusses other print media, including magazines and trade journals. Finally, it presents important information on radio and television.

Approaching the Media—Some Initial Advice

As we have seen in the previous chapter, to work successfully with the media you must first decide what your message is and whom you want to reach with that message. Then you must identify which media sources are most likely to reach that audience. For example, if you're going after a young audience, focus on radio stations, weekly newspapers, campus media, local TV news, and the Internet. If you want to persuade or inform legislators or policy makers, go after newspapers with wide circulations and public broadcasting. If you want to reach a certain geographical area, go after all the media in that area—TV, radio, and local publications, such as magazines, newspapers, and weeklies.

Print, TV, and radio each have different requirements when it comes to deciding what makes news. Understanding what is newsworthy for each media outlet is key to pitching your news story. Put most simply, TV needs pictures, radio needs voices, and print needs quotes. Organizing a news conference with a medical device demonstration is good for TV. Having the developer of the device answer questions provides good quotes in print. Have a number of story angles, and choose your targets accordingly.

If you have sent out a news release (see Chapter 4), you may want to follow up with a call. Ask if the reporter received your release and whether or not you could have two minutes of his or her time to explain the contents of the release. Reporters are always busy—so get to the point. They receive hundreds of story suggestions each week. Reporters have good news judgment and can often decide within a moment or two whether or not they are interested in your idea.

If the reporter says no, more often than not it means no. Express your thanks and move on. If the reporter likes your story idea, you're halfway to getting coverage; but you still have work to do. Reporters will often ask for background information and contact names. Make sure you have them on hand. Media outlets with daily deadlines need information quickly. Whether or not you have it available can decide whether the story runs or not.

Remember that once you attract media attention, you can't always control how it will turn out, what message will be communicated, what "spin" the reporter will put on things, who the reporter might contact to verify or complement the information you've provided, or how far the reporter might dig.

The Print Media

It's highly likely that most of your public relations efforts will be directed to print media. This is simply a matter of numbers. There are many more print outlets—local newspapers, weekly magazines, trade publications, association newsletters—than there are broadcast outlets. Furthermore, while much of the work of the profession is visual and therefore suitable for television coverage, the varied lengths and formats of the print media provide a better opportunity for coverage than short, one- to three-minute broadcast stories.

This section begins by summarizing some important information about working with the print media. The subsequent sections concern specific types of print media—newspapers, magazines, and trade journals.

Editors: The Key Players

The editor is the person responsible for selecting print news. He or she may be responsible for an entire publication or for a single department. Every editor may not have the intellectual prowess or influence that the head of *The New York Times* has; however, all editors do have the same basic responsibility—to find news or feature material to meet their readers' interests and needs, to prepare it for publication according to the publication's style and format, and to publish it. This process must be done with fresh material every day, week, or month, depending upon the frequency of the publication.

With rare exceptions, there is a high, thick wall between a publication's advertising and editorial departments. If that wall is sometimes breached, it's never through an open door. Few publications, and none of any editorial quality, will provide publicity in exchange for advertising. Therefore, the fact that you may be a major advertiser in any publication does not entitle you to breach its editorial independence. Your news or feature material stands on its merits alone.

While it is true that advertisers sometimes have greater access to editorial pages than do nonadvertisers, any publication that allows its advertising department to influence its editorial department will soon lose its readers and its credibility. And since the value of editorial publicity is the implied "third party" independent endorsement, using advertising clout for editorial space can be self-defeating. Even in smaller publications such as community newspapers or penny savers, in which the practice of catering to advertisers is fairly common, the news should still be capable of standing on its own.

When dealing with an editor, the important thing to remember is that the editor's responsibility is to give his or her readers what they want to read. What is consistent with the editor's needs is not always consistent with yours. The techniques of publicity are designed to make your needs consistent with those of the editor.

Editorial Board Meetings

An editorial meeting—whether it is with an editorial board or a single editorial writer—is a unique opportunity for pharmacists to present their viewpoints on health issues to the print media and broadcast outlets. Unlike hard news, editorials present opinions. Editorials often follow news events. Your opportunity to promote editorial coverage will be enhanced by the amount of hard news coverage your activities have received in the community. Pharmacists can take advantage of editorial meetings to turn the media's attention to the urgent need of healthcare in America.

Always remember that when you meet with an editorial board or any newspaper staff, you are meeting on its turf. The newspaper is extending you a courtesy by listening to and considering your point of view. Return the courtesy by respecting the editorial board's opinions, positions, and constraints. For example, before you meet with the editorial board, make sure you know what the paper has written on your subject in the past. This preparation is good, but it is also common courtesy. It will help you tailor your case to the special interests of your target audience—the editorial board.

To help you prepare, it's a good idea to keep files on what your local papers have written on issues of importance to you *and* to them. Such a filing system can be very useful in preparing for meetings with representatives of the papers. While you may have kept a file on your issues, you may not be aware of what position the paper has taken on others— for example, physician-assisted suicide or patient confidentiality. It is especially important to read the paper on the day of your meeting. If an article about your issue or your organization has appeared in the paper that day, people on the editorial board will expect you to have read it.

Prepare a one-page fact sheet in support of your position, and bring enough copies for everyone in the meeting. Also bring copies of any information on your issue and the names and phone numbers of people who can be contacted for more information.

You might be tempted to bring other experts with you to the meeting, but a good general rule is the smaller the group, the better. Some advise that going alone is often the best approach to presenting the necessary information and answering most questions from the editorial staff. You can always get back to the board later with information or answers that you did not have at the meeting.

A typical editorial board meeting starts with your opportunity to state your case. Your opening statement should be limited to a few minutes. It should summarize your position on the issue, the evidence that supports this position, the anticipated criticisms of your opponents, and appropriate responses to those criticisms.

Once you have stated your case, expect questions. Not all the questions will seem friendly, even if the board is predisposed to agree with you. This is because editorial boards must consider the counterarguments they will receive from their readers. Board members often want to test the validity of your position by playing the role of devil's advocate. It is crucial to anticipate the most common criticisms of your position and be prepared to defend against them. Practice your responses; if you wish, prepare note cards with key points. The way in which you respond to questions is as important as the way in which you make your original case. After all, if you can't adequately defend your opinions, how can the newspaper be expected to defend them?

It is always useful to be prepared with the names and phone numbers of those opponents with whose comments you are willing to live. For example, if you inventory in your mind all those groups that are likely to attack your position, identify the ones you find easiest to counteract. In other words, be prepared to give ground but not to arm your enemies. You don't need to give the editorial board the names of people who will undermine your credibility. Left to their own devices, the board members will simply go through their source list. So stack the deck yourself rather than trust random selection.

If the newspaper decides not to do an editorial or takes an editorial stance that is contrary to your position, suggest that it print an op-ed piece or a letter to the editor (see Chapter 4) from your organization. Do not offer such an alternative unless you are sure the newspaper won't run an editorial. But being prepared with this option can help save the situation.

If the editors decide not to agree with you, make it clear that agreement on any particular issue is not a prerequisite for maintaining an ongoing relationship of mutual respect. Remember, there will always be another issue down the road.

Reporters and Beats

Each division of a large newspaper has its own staff editor in addition to general assignment reporters and reporters who have specialties or beats. These beats may include banking, retailing, transportation, and taxes in the business section; architecture and design in the home section; local education and city planning in the metro section; and movie and book reviews in the lifestyle section. These reporters may also be supported by bureaus in major cities, wire service bureaus, or news services. Some may be freelance writers. Many newspapers have health reporters or editors; some even produce a separate section devoted to health. Some editors do both editing and reporting.

One of your primary jobs in initiating a public relations campaign is to identify the reporter who covers your beat—that is, pharmacy and health issues. This task entails compiling and updating a media list, as described in Chapter 2. Then, if you think your news is just right for a particular newspaper or magazine columnist, call or write that person directly. There is no need to send materials to an editor first.

Articles written by national newspaper columnists are generally distributed by syndication. Some of these reporters may be contacted by writing to them in care of the local publication in which their column appears. Call your local paper first to confirm that the letter will be forwarded, or ask someone at the newspaper for the address of the syndication service that distributes that particular columnist.

Reporters usually request that a story be offered to them on an exclusive basis. This means you will not give the story to anyone else until after the columnist uses it or turns down the idea. If you are offering a story as an exclusive, a follow-up phone call is vital. If the first person to whom you send the material is not interested, you can then offer it to another columnist exclusively or send it out for general release. If one of the columnists to whom you offer it wishes to use it, wait until the column has appeared. You are then free to send out the same materials for general release.

Deadlines

To work well with the media, you must understand the pressures under which they operate. None of these pressures is stronger than deadlines.

Most print reporters and editors work a fairly regular schedule. For morning newspapers, this generally means they work 10 a.m. to 7 p.m. While the largest number of staff work Monday through Friday, news people are on duty on weekends as well and a skeleton crew staffs the newsroom throughout the night. For afternoon and evening papers, reporters and editors can often be found in their offices as early as 7 a.m. Morning newspaper reporters working on a health feature, for example, generally work a normal day. Should they decide to attend a news conference, they would prefer to do so before the middle of the day. Once they are into the afternoon, they generally work toward a deadline of between 5 p.m. and 7 p.m.

Magazines and trade publications usually maintain Monday through Friday, 9 a.m. to 5 p.m., schedules. Be sure to check with each publication with which you work to make sure that you coordinate with their work schedules.

To be aware of these schedules is to be aware of the problems of media deadlines.

Newspapers

There is not a community in the United States that isn't served by a newspaper of some kind, and three quarters of all adults read newspapers. Newspapers are widely read by people of all ages, economic status, and education. Their journalistic quality ranges from the meticulous professionalism of the influential big-city papers, such as *The New York Times* and *The St. Louis Post-Dispatch*, to the sometimes-casual style of small-town weeklies.

Larger cities may have two competing newspapers and sometimes a morning and an evening paper. Smaller cities and towns usually have one daily paper for the city and in some cases a county or areawide paper. In many cases, people in small communities subscribe both to a local paper and to the newspaper from the nearest major city.

Because newspapers have the broadest news coverage, they are the prime outlets for distribution of publicity material. Names of reporters and editors from your town's local daily newspaper, the major newspaper in a nearby city, regional papers, and any weekly neighborhood or community papers in your area should be on your media list.

Print Media

TOP TIPS

Newspapers have numerous reporters covering special beats— the main news section, the editorial page, op-ed opinion pieces, letters to the editor, the business section, consumer news, and the style section offering soft news.

Make a list of business editors, reporters covering health, and other journalists who can tell your story and direct your material to the correct person. This will greatly increase the likelihood that it will be used.

Don't overlook weekly newspapers, "shoppers," and penny savers. The latter two are mainly advertising vehicles for local merchants; however, these papers are usually looking for editorial material.

As noted earlier, major newspapers are organized by departments, and each department is responsible for assembling certain sections of the paper. Your first step is to determine the appropriate section to contact. Look for a regular byline in that section or call and ask for the name of the editor of that section.

America's Top 30 Newspapers

Wall Street Journal
USA Today
The New York Times
Los Angeles Times
Washington Post
New York Daily News
Chicago Tribune
Newsday
Houston Chronicle
Chicago Sun-Times
San Francisco Chronicle
Dallas Morning News
Boston Globe
Arizona Republic
New York Post
Philadelphia Inquirer
Newark Star-Ledger
Detroit Free Press
Cleveland Plain Dealer
San Diego Union-Tribune
Orange County Register
Miami Herald
Portland Oregonian
Denver Post
St. Petersburg Times
St. Louis Post-Dispatch
Baltimore Sun
Rocky Mountain News
Atlanta Constitution
San Jose Mercury News

Source: Audit Bureau of Circulations 9/97.

Neighborhood or community newspapers are usually put out weekly by very small staffs. Their quietest day—and, therefore, the best day for phoning them—is the day their paper is distributed. Photographs generally increase your chance of coverage here. A story of particular significance to community residents has the best chance of being picked up.

News and Wire Services

A news or wire service is a news outlet that tracks stories that are then wired by computer throughout a city, region, state, or country. Working with the news services is a great way of maximizing the number of outlets that place your story. If an outlet doesn't cover a story directly, it may use the wire service version.

When pitching a story to a news service, start with the assignment editor or ask the switchboard operator for the appropriate contact for the issue you're addressing.

A daybook is a calendar of events that is distributed to reporters daily through a news service. Daybook editors should receive your media advisory (see Chapter 4), which contains the "who, what, when, and why" of a media event.

The major news services are:

Associated Press (AP) is the oldest and largest wire service in the world. It has nearly 240 news bureaus worldwide. AP supplies news to thousands of newspapers, electronic media, and publications.

Find out whether there is an AP bureau in your city. If not, the bureau in the nearest largest city will usually be responsible for covering your area's activities. Call and get the name of the person to contact should the need arise. You can also check the Internet for "Wire Services and News Sources."

Business Wire offers specialty news, business news, and news releases with a global reach.

Dow-Jones is interested primarily in business and financial news. This wire goes to investment houses, brokerages, banks, and other members of the financial community as well as to the media.

Knight Ridder/Tribune News Services is the most popular supplemental wire service and is famous for great informational graphics.

New York Times Syndicate is a limited but high-quality news service drawn from some specialized *New York Times* content.

Reuters is strong in international and specialty news. It is a sophisticated wire service.

Scripps Howard News Service, once available only to Scripps papers, has become a full service wire available to media everywhere.

United Press International (UPI) was once a strong competitor to AP. UPI is now a struggling smaller player in the scheme of news services. It supplies news to thousands of newspapers, electronic media, and publications throughout the world.

Magazines

Like newspapers, magazines are organized by department. At major publications, different editors oversee different departments, while at smaller publications, one editor or managing editor generally oversees everything.

There are two categories of consumer magazines that might interest pharmacists: city or regional magazines and national magazines.

City and regional magazines are a natural outlet for healthcare feature material because of their geographic distribution and their editorial slant. The narrower the geographic distribution, the greater the likelihood that the editors will be interested in news and feature material from a local source. These publications offer the opportunity for general feature materials, citing you as a source, on such subjects as local healthcare trends, specific diseases (e.g., how to manage asthma), what you should know about your medications, and similar topics.

National magazines, including news magazines such as *Time* and *Newsweek*, are interested in only the most unusual healthcare news. They are, however, interested in stories about pharmacy as long as they are relevant to their readers.

If you're seeking magazine coverage, begin by becoming familiar with its departments, the nature of the news it covers, and the length and tone of its articles. You may find a writer who seems like the right person to receive your particular information. If so, get in touch. Staff writers can be contacted by writing or phoning the publication. If you suspect that a particular writer is a freelancer, you can sometimes contact him or her by sending a letter in care of the publication. You could also call to get a phone number and address.

If no one writer seems right for receiving your materials, call the publication to get the name of an editor to whom your information could be sent.

Some magazines will not consider unsolicited material but will follow up on ideas suggested to them. If you think you might have such a story, try to develop specific approaches suitable for a particular publication.

In other cases, magazines do accept unsolicited articles. If that's true for a publication on your target list, you may write an article and submit it for consideration. An article on "Questions to Ask Your Pharmacist" under your byline in *Good Housekeeping* magazine can quickly make you a national authority.

Track magazine deadlines closely when mailing time-oriented materials. Depending on the production schedule, magazines close anywhere from two weeks to four months ahead of publication time. Call to learn the schedule of the magazines on your media list.

Trade Journals

Trade journals rely heavily on publicity sources for news. If the readers of a pharmacy trade journal are in any way a part of your potential target, these publications can be an excellent publicity outlet.

PERSONAL EXAMPLE

Creating Story Ideas

I had scheduled a meeting between health editors from *Woman's Day* magazine in New York and two national pharmacy figures. This was the first time that we had met one-on-one with this consumer publication. We took the two editors to a restaurant for lunch where we could exchange information in an informal atmosphere.

As we were waiting for our lunch, the pharmacists began discussing pharmacy issues such as the changing role of the pharmacist and pharmaceutical care. The editors reached for their notebooks and began taking notes. They found these issues so interesting and important to their readers that they created several short pieces on what had been discussed that day.

Some better-known pharmacy trade journals include:

▶ *Chain Drug Review*
220 Fifth Avenue
New York, NY 10001
(212) 213-6000

▶ *Drug Store News*
425 Park Avenue
New York, NY 10022
(212) 756-5000

▶ *Drug Topics*
5 Paragon Drive
Montvale, NJ 07645
(201) 358-7200

▶ *The Green Sheet*
5550 Friendship Boulevard
Chevy Chase, MD 20815
(301) 657-9830

▶ *Health News Daily*
5550 Friendship Boulevard
Chevy Chase, MD 20815
(301) 657-9830

▶ *Pharmacy Times*
1065 Old Country Road
Westbury, NY 11590
(516) 997-0377

▶ *The Pink Sheet*
5550 Friendship Boulevard
Chevy Chase, MD 20815
(301) 657-9830

▶ *Supermarket News*
7 West 34th Street
New York, NY 10001
(212) 630-3770

▶ *U.S. Pharmacist*
100 Avenue of the Americas
New York, NY 10013
(212) 274-7000

Other Print Media

Other vehicles for publicity consist of any media distributed to the public. Such publications include the house organs and newsletters of other companies and the journals of fraternal and church organizations.

Don't forget the so-called penny savers and shoppers. Thousands of these publications are distributed throughout the country at shopping centers and supermarkets, as well as door to door. They usually include editorial material in addition to advertising. The editorial material frequently is chatty and loaded with items of interest to community residents. They are a natural outlet for publicity.

Working with TV Producers and Reporters

Television has the largest audience of all the media. It reaches all segments of the population. Television is America's primary source of news and information. According to the U.S. Census in 1990, more than 98% of all homes have television sets. On the average, a person spends more than 7 hours a day watching television.

Television has the ability to grab attention and create appeal through the combination of pictures, sound, and motion. Since television is visual, anything you can show or demonstrate is a selling point when contacting television talk shows or news programs. If your story does not have visual appeal, you may want to consider targeting it to the print media.

Television stations, except for the smaller ones and cable TV, devote remarkably little time to news—and particularly to news of activities that concern very few people. Moreover, television news coverage is rarely in depth: it usually reduces complex stories to 30- or 60-second segments. Some stations might pick up events or feature material that would add a human interest angle to a newscast. That depends, however, on how heavy the news day has been. Because of these limitations, if it could be quantified, television as a publicity outlet ranks a poor third after newspapers and radio.

Pitching a Story to a TV Producer

Before a professional publicist makes a pitch to the media, he or she usually first identifies the person in charge at the targeted media outlet and sends along a media kit (see Chapter 4). If you want to pitch a story to a TV station, your contact should be the news director or assignment editor. For talk shows, it is the host or producer of the show. For public service programming, contact the public service director.

The key to a "cold call" to an assignment editor is to have a news package that mixes hard news with visual elements. Your chances are better if you have cultivated a relationship with the assignment editor or the correspondent who covers your issue. If you know a producer or researcher, that may also help. Begin the call by stating your name and asking whether the person has received your media kit. Then ask if it's a good time to talk. If so, continue with words such as the following:

"I have a unique health segment I think you might be interested in."

"I specialize in the healthcare field and there is an important new [product, service] that I think might help your viewers to _____."

"Perhaps you've seen the recent articles in *Newsweek* and *USA Today* on _____. I think you might be interested in following up this national story with a local story on _____."

If you have a good clip file (related stories clipped from the print media) on your story, and the story is visual enough to make good television, you have a better chance of getting the attention of a producer or assignment editor. You may include this in the media kit or send it later to follow up on your conversation.

Personalize the story as much as possible. Show how the issue or special event affects the life of people in your community. Emphasize the impact of the issue on the quality, access, and cost of healthcare, on jobs, or on the economy of the region.

Getting to Yes

Producers appreciate enthusiasm and want to be convinced that you are offering them a good media story. They want to feel that you are knowledgeable and that you understand their needs and those of their viewers.

It's also their job to ask questions and probe deeper to make sure they understand your story. Don't be put off by an initial lack of interest or a comment such as, "We don't usually use this kind of story." Objections are standard operating procedure in television. You are being tested. The media

PERSONAL EXAMPLE

Give Them What They Want

When working with the media, it's important to give them what they want. For years, as part of the American Pharmaceutical Association's Annual Meeting, we held an officers' briefing. The purpose was to give the media an opportunity to meet with APhA leaders and ask questions. Although these briefings were well attended by the media, especially the pharmacy trades, there had been very little interaction among the participants and the media in recent years.

I polled the media participants individually to find out why the dynamics of the briefing had changed over the years. They admitted that they were not going to ask questions and give their competitors the edge to know what they were going to write about. They wanted to write exclusive stories, and they could not ask the questions they needed to ask in a group setting.

We stopped holding an officers' briefing and began to schedule one-on-one briefings with the media during the Annual Meeting. That proved very successful. The media had their exclusive stories, and APhA was able to get its leadership in front of the key media who could get out the message.

So make sure that you don't do things the same way just because you've always done it that way, especially if you're not achieving the results you had in mind. The media are not shy. Just ask them what they want. They will surely tell you. And you can make adjustments in your programs that will benefit all parties.

person wants to know if you are a good source: savvy and dependable. They want to be convinced you are knowledgeable enough to judge a good story, guest, or segment. They also want to be convinced you have good follow-through and will deliver all elements on time.

Be flexible. Approach the idea with slightly different facts and information. Tell them who else is interested, how many people will be affected, what visuals you have to offer, and why this is newsworthy.

It may also help to ask the producer what it would take to persuade her to use your idea. Listen. It's a great way to learn. It gives you an opportunity to overcome objections and helps you discover what does appeal. Each station and producer are different and have different needs and requirements. Be prepared to customize your standard information. Don't give up without a polite fight.

Television people understand the importance of being first to get information to the viewers. You'd be surprised how media people can move things around when they get interested in an idea. There is a constant reshuffling of the schedule in an effort to be current. When times are slow, your "sell" will be easier. When times are fast, you'd better be hot!

At any rate, once you've done your best to convince the editor of the value of your story, be content with his or her decision. At most

TOP TIPS

Identifying Broadcast Media

Begin with the local affiliates of the major national networks. While you may seldom have news or features of interest to a national network, these channels and stations function as local outlets. Television stations have local news programs, editorial opinions and "talk back" opportunities, public affairs programs, one-on-one interview shows, and public affairs specials. Call to find out the names of the assignment editors, news editors, and producers of local interview and talk shows.

Community cable stations offer local news programming, community access channels, and public affairs programming.

Public television stations provide local news programming as well as a diverse mix of locally produced public affairs programming.

Radio formats include all-news stations, talk shows, public affairs programming, and editorial comment.

local stations, the decisions of the assignment editor or the news editor are final. Thank them for the opportunity to talk and note that you hope to be in touch again with a story that might be better suited to their audience.

Next Steps

Once you've gotten a TV producer interested in your story, a reporter may come to you or the station may invite you to the studio for an interview.

In either case, the motto is "Be prepared." If a news director or assignment editor likes your idea and says the station will send out a crew, find out whether they expect anything specific. By learning the angle they intend to take, you will be better prepared for their arrival.

If a producer or host invites you to come to the studio to be a guest on a talk show, ask about the length of your segment, the subject to be discussed, whether you will be appearing alone or as part of a panel, and whether the segment will be taped or live. Also ask whom you should contact on arrival.

Try to ensure that the interviewer knows something about the profession before you go on air. Stress beforehand that pharmacists are an important part of the healthcare team, working with the physician and the patient to provide optimal care. Explain how nonadherence with medication instructions drives up healthcare costs through increased hospitalization and emergency room visits, as well as driving up employers' costs when prolonged illnesses keep people off work. This briefing can be accomplished politely and quickly just before the interview.

If the TV crew films on site, encourage the producer or reporter to show you counseling a patient (preferably in front of the counter), reviewing a medication profile on the computer, or talking to a physician on the telephone. If they ask to shoot you "counting and pouring," explain that such a picture is not representative of a pharmacist's work—it is a distributive function that does not require the expertise of a pharmacist. If the story is focusing on a certain medication and they want a representative visual, suggest they show you or the patient holding the prescription vial while you are interacting with the patient.

If you are in the television studio for the interview, wear business attire—a suit and tie for a man or a business dress or suit for a woman. Solid colors are best. Stay away from busy patterns that distract viewers. Black and white are also to be avoided, as they appear too harsh. A light blue shirt usually is best for a man.

Finally, accept the fact that every interview may not result in a story and every story that gets written may not be exactly the story you want to see published. Every interview will, however, build your self-confidence and make the next one go more smoothly.

Pitching a Health Story to a TV Network

If you find yourself in the position of pitching a story to a national network, the procedure is the same; however, the pressure and questioning may be greater. Suppose, for example, that you are a pharmacist who heads a team that has just developed a promising new medication. Here are the types of questions you would probably receive.

How is this better than what is available? If it doesn't improve, it's not news. Media have no interest in "me, too" treatments.

Is it a small improvement in a large population or a dramatic improvement in a narrow disease? Both types of stories can make news. If the disease affects few people, the personal story of a patient and his or her dramatic responses to treatment are what will make it work for a program such as *20/20*. If it is a condition that affects huge numbers, like osteoporosis, media want something new, a new study, a new drug, and a new diagnostic tool. They keep up with medical news and usually have a good idea of what is news for the public.

How many patients are affected? Editors want to know how many patients have the disease and how many might potentially use the new therapy. The number usually has to be large, unless there is a very dramatic impact.

Where is the treatment in the FDA approval process? Editors today are becoming more knowledgeable about drug approval. They are looking more often at earlier phases, and if it is something really exciting and it's being tested overseas, they certainly may be interested. Previously they only did stories about treatments that were approved or near approval, but increasingly they are looking at interesting treatments in earlier stages of the process. They always would like early warnings on treatments nearing FDA approval.

Who are the leading investigators? With what institutions are they affiliated? What previous coverage has this story received? If the story has been on *Dateline NBC*, the editors of *20/20* won't even consider it. If the story has had no coverage, it may be harder to evaluate, but the media always love "exclusives" and reporting something important first. If an evening news program from a network competitor has done the story, they need a new angle or a hook for their evening news, and even then, chances are slim. Staff will do a "news research check" on stories that look promising to see if they have been covered. You can advance your chances significantly by doing that check for them.

What will the viewer see? TV producers need patients, at a minimum, but often that is not enough. They need to show the treatment working—or show the severity of the disease (for example, the patient with cluster headaches who beats his head against the wall or the treatment that restores a patient's voice). If there are no dramatic pictures of the treatment or the effect, is there interesting high-tech diagnostic equipment or dramatic magnetic resonance images?

TV Talk Shows

TV talk shows, both local and syndicated, are increasingly popular, and their hosts are always on the lookout for new guests. Appearing on such a show, either as a single guest or part of a panel, is a great way to break into TV. Here are some tips on how to schedule and conduct TV talk show appearances.

Know the show's format and provide a compelling reason to appear on the show. A producer's main objective is to attract and sustain an audience. Your goal is to promote yourself as an expert with a unique angle.

Emphasize your expertise. Television producers agree that the most important characteristic a potential guest must have is credibility. What are the keys to convincing producers that you are credible? Send a brief bio sketch, magazine and newspaper clippings, background on your practice, and a listing of radio and television interviews you have conducted. Offer anything that makes the producer feel comfortable that you can speak in front of the camera, including a videotape of your appearance on other TV talk shows.

Tie your comments into a current news angle. Producers like guests who are able to speak about current, hot news. Ask yourself the following questions: What are the big health news stories driving the news? What makes you qualified to discuss these stories? Don't make the mistake of trying to sell a producer an angle that is really nothing more than an advertisement for your practice.

TOP TIPS

TV Interviews

Never enter an interview without knowing your objectives. If you get a spontaneous phone call from a reporter, the best way to handle it is to call the person back after you have had a chance to think about the key objectives you want to convey.

If you want something to be "off the record," get a formal guarantee of anonymity in advance from the interviewer.

Try to drive an interview rather than let it be driven for you. Answer questions by bringing them back to the points you want to emphasize.

Take every opportunity to underline your key objectives.

Say the word "pharmacist" early and often. For example, answer a question by saying, "Pharmacists are trained in..." or "As a pharmacist I am often asked to..."

Before the day of the interview, submit suggested questions you can address. Offer real-life examples that mesh with your subject. You'll make your interviewer feel more knowledgeable and at ease and, perhaps, create the basis for a continuing relationship.

Radio: Tried and True

Radio audiences are more targeted than TV audiences. For this reason, it is important that you pitch your story to the right station. For example, it is highly unlikely that a rock station, with its young audience, would be interested in a story about hormone replacement therapy. But if the story is about a new cure for acne, the rock station might be interested. It is important to understand their different audiences and tailor your messages accordingly.

Radio can get your message to the largest number of people when you have an urgent message to convey which requires immediate action. A majority of local radio stations have regular news segments throughout the day. Some rely on news syndicates to cover community events while some have reporters to cover the news. Larger stations in big markets have fully staffed news operations. Having local or regional news angles is essential in most talk radio programs. If your issue is relevant to the listeners, you can expect good radio coverage.

It is essential to recognize that radio is the prime source for breaking news. Radio stations need information as the event takes place. They must get the information before the newspapers have used it. Once it appears in print, the news value is gone.

PERSONAL EXAMPLE

Interviewing Made Easy: Answer Your Own Questions!

Several former clients of mine made very interesting subjects for the talk show circuit. In some cases, because they were so different—a major caterer, an author, a realtor, a lady racecar driver—I was sometimes able to book more than one on the same day on a local talk show.

When sending a pitch letter to the producer, I always included a series of potential questions the guest could address. Nine times out of ten, the show simply reproduced these questions on the teleprompter for the host to read. The guest went through the interview with great ease. But you can't always count on this. You must be prepared for any question from out of the blue.

To pitch a story to a radio station, begin by compiling a list of potential target stations. You can get a complete listing of all the AM and FM stations in your area from the newspaper. Get the phone numbers and addresses from the telephone book.

Listen to a particular program before submitting material. Determine why you would be a good guest and what you would like to talk about. Then find out who is in charge of scheduling guests for a talk show (producer, host, or talent coordinator) or in charge of making assignments for a news program (news director or assignment editor).

If you wish to call, once you have the reporter or newscaster on the phone, don't waste time. Get to the point. Explain why the story is important, why the audience will be interested in it, and what you have to offer—perhaps a phone feed and a local expert the station can follow up with for a supporting opinion.

Or, if you are writing the radio station in advance, develop a radio media kit. This kit can be as simple as a media alert and a news release (see Chapter 4). You may also wish to include a cover letter explaining the news value and angle of the story, an actuality on tape, a fact sheet with additional information, the names and phone numbers of your experts, and a brief backgrounder on each person. Or you can include all the necessary information in a letter. If you don't know the news director's name, just address it to News Director. It will be reviewed.

Once you've sent the materials, follow up. Contact the station 24 hours in advance to see if they will take a feed or an actuality on the day of the event, and, if so, confirm the time. An actuality is a tape recording with a voice-over opening and closing; in between is a statement from a spokesperson or expert discussing the subject. The station may use the introduction as is or use its own staff anchor or announcer for the introduction and closing. If you're calling about a news conference, arrange for the feed to take place shortly after the conference ends. A feed is an electronic signal sent from the source to other outlets.

News anchors or commentators at some stations do their own editing and make decisions on what goes on the air. Try to determine who these individuals are and when they are on the air. If you have a story to pitch, don't call during air time or an hour or so before. If they are on in the afternoon, they will be at the station in the morning. Call then.

If the story is breaking news, fax a media alert and follow up with a phone call. If your story is not breaking news, lead time is essential. If you have an important event coming up, give your contact some advance notice, such as a few days for a news conference. Call about 45 days in advance to pitch a booking for a planned event.

Keeping in Touch

Regardless of whether the story is good news or bad, always say thank you. Continue to update reporters on the successes of your project and provide statistics on any changes in your community's health that can be traced to your program.

Summary

Achieving good coverage for your organization and generating interest in its activities requires time, imagination, courtesy, and attention to detail.

Persistence is the final ingredient for successful contact with the media. Sometimes a publication will like your idea immediately. The first thing you know, a word-for-word copy of your news release will appear in the local paper. On other occasions, they won't be interested. Perhaps you need to wait a month and send the reporter or editor an updated version of the same news release. You may need to come up with a completely new angle for your next approach. Intuition and common sense will be your best guides in each situation. It may take several calls to a television or radio station before you give them a story angle they want to pursue.

Persistence *will* pay off. If you stick with it and keep trying different approaches, you will find that there's a way to get into almost every media outlet you want.▶

CHAPTER 4

Basic Media Tools

Public relations, as we've seen, is the sum of a great many factors—all of which are designed to give the public a favorable impression about you and your practice. It's an ongoing attitude that should pervade every aspect of your work.

To create this favorable attitude, you must be able to use a variety of publicity tools. These tools include written materials, such as pitch letters, news releases, and public service announcements. They also include events such as news conferences and public presentations.

This chapter describes the tools you can use to communicate to your publics through the media. You may not need to use all of them to promote your practice. It's up to you to decide which ones would be most effective to achieve your goals.

The Pitch Letter

The pitch letter is one of the primary tools of communication with the media. You can use a pitch letter to introduce yourself to an editor or a producer. You can use it to suggest feature stories, set up interviews, and obtain coverage for news conferences and special events.

The rules that apply to the format of a news release (discussed later) do not apply to a pitch letter. The pitch letter permits a greater use of your imagination and initiative.

Write your pitch letter as you would any business letter, using your business stationery. Leave plenty of white space. Use several short paragraphs, rather than a few long ones. Make the letter lively and persuasive. Unless the story you are pitching is of world-shaking importance, keep your letter to a page or a page and a half. News people are deluged with mail and have a sharp eye for unnecessary padding.

Use the opening lines to grab the reader's attention and introduce the entire concept of the story. Beyond that, just answer the reporter's basic questions: who, what, when, where, why, and how. In addition, you may wish to list the material you have available: screenings, health information, and so forth. Offer an interview on your story subject with an expert, if there is one available.

Be sure that your name and phone number appear prominently. If there are specific hours when you can be reached, include that information in the letter. Be imaginative, be creative, but, above all, be persistent. Keep sending out those letters. If one editor rejects them, try another. If one idea seems not to work, then try another.

Sample Pitch Letter

Date

Name of Journalist
Name of Publication
Street Address
City, State, Zip Code

Dear Mr./Ms. [Last Name]:

With the growing concern throughout the country about healthcare, I am writing for your help in publicizing several events that will benefit your readers'/viewers' health. [YOUR PHARMACY] has launched a campaign to make sure the community is medicating safely and effectively.

The public has ready access to information about medications from their pharmacists, but many times they are not aware that this advice can make a difference in their health.

Health Events for the upcoming week include:

"Brown Bag" Medicine Review
October 00, 9 a.m. to 5 p.m., [YOUR PHARMACY, STREET ADDRESS, CITY]. The public is asked to bring in all their medicines for a checkup. Pharmacists will be available for a personal consultation to ensure that the individual is not taking or storing expired medications and is not taking medications that, when taken together, could cause adverse effects.

Free Diabetes Screenings
October 00, 10 a.m. to 3 p.m. Screenings will be provided by medical personnel at [YOUR PHARMACY, STREET ADDRESS, CITY]. Information on the disease will be provided.

Free Blood Pressure Checks
October 00, 10 a.m. to 12 p.m. Have your blood pressure checked by a pharmacist at [YOUR PHARMACY, STREET ADDRESS, CITY]. Receive information on how to prevent high blood pressure.

Free Glaucoma Screenings
October 00, 3 to 5 p.m. These screenings will be provided by [PHYSICIAN] and his/her staff at [YOUR PHARMACY, STREET ADDRESS, CITY].

Community Forum on the Inappropriate Use of Prescribed Medications
October 00, 6 to 7 p.m. Join the [YOUR ORGANIZATION] for this community health forum in [LOCATION]. The discussion will be lead by [PHARMACIST], and will include a video presentation and overview of the changing role of the pharmacist.

Community Health Fair
October 00, 9 a.m. to 1 p.m. Join pharmacists, nurses, doctors, dieticians, and exercise specialists at [LOCATION] and receive information for a healthier you.

Hotline on Pain Management: (800) 000-0000
October 00, 9 a.m. to 6 p.m. Call the toll-free number and talk to a pharmacist with any questions you have about pain relievers. The hotline is sponsored by [YOUR ORGANIZATION].

I will be following up by telephone soon to see if you are interested in additional information on any of the above events. In the meantime, please feel free to contact me at (000) 000-0000 if I can be of assistance.

Sincerely,

Name
Title

Media Kits

A media kit is a collection of print materials, assembled in a folder, that describes your organization, its services, and other relevant information. One big advantage of a media kit is flexibility. You may add materials to the kit or delete materials from it, depending on the audience. Media kits are essential elements of news conferences.

Media kits are inexpensive and easy to prepare. If compiled correctly, they can be used to "package" an entire issue—complete with graphics, sidebars, and other relevant background materials. Include items in the kit that reinforce your story, such as other news clips about the project, photos, pertinent news releases, fact sheets (with statistics on the implications of medication misuse, for example), brochures, and other hard data that reporters will find helpful. Be sure to include photocopies of articles that have been written about your pharmacy. A résumé summarizing your background is helpful, too; be sure to list presentations you've made and articles you've published. Include your business card.

Place these items in a folder with pockets. These folders should bear a label with the name of your organization, pharmacy, hospital, or business. You can also have folders printed or use stickers with your name and logo.

News Releases

A news release is a summary of details concerning an event or key points about an issue of importance to you and your publics. Issue a news release whenever you have something important to say: the start of a new program; a change in an existing program that will affect many people; the appointment of a new staff member; the results of a program or study. You can also use a news release to clarify your position on a timely issue.

Some Basics

To be sure that your release gets into the proper hands, it's best to have it hand delivered or faxed to the editor; however, U.S. mail can also be used if the issue is not urgent or extremely important.

Once a news release has been prepared, it can be inserted into a media kit of background materials. Often when your news is not pressing or significant enough to warrant a news conference or media briefing (discussed later), you should still send out a news release.

If you send out several news releases a year, you may want to have a special news release letterhead printed. You can include "News" or "News Release" in colored ink across the top or bottom of the paper. It is also perfectly acceptable to send your news releases out on your regular business letterhead.

Ensuring Your Release is Read

Although news releases are convenient and cost effective for the sender, it is hard to guarantee that they will have the desired effect. Newsrooms are inundated with news releases. The average editor may receive several hundred of them in a typical week. Only 10–20% are used in some way. How can you increase the chances that your release will be in that lucky 10–20%?

The first rule of "trash can avoidance" is obvious: Don't send trash! Prepare your news release meticulously.

Second, don't bury the recipients in a paper blizzard. Send news releases only when you have something worth an editor's time. An editor who receives too many releases with too little news value soon learns to ignore everything that comes from that source.

Finally, to ensure that your news release will be read, present it in classic news release format. The format is designed to give a straightforward presentation of your story. Its key parts are a good, clear headline and a concise introductory paragraph that tells the editor the all-important

Writing a News Release

TOP TIPS

Have the release typed on one side of a standard 8½ x 11-inch paper. Use double spacing.

Use black ink and standard typefaces.

Leave ample margins and sufficient space at the top and bottom for editors to make notes.

At the top right side of the first page, supply the name and phone number of the contact person who can offer more detailed information on the topic or event.

Use a headline (capital letters and bold type) to summarize the story and grab the attention of the editor.

Identify the city and state of origin of your release at the beginning of the release in caps.

Keep the release to one page if possible. For a longer release, place -more- at the bottom center of each page. At the top of continuing pages, write, for example, *Page 2 – Medication Tips.*

Conclude with a paragraph indicating what you want the reader, listener or viewer to do as a result of reading or hearing about your story. For example, "Call for more information: 555-5555," or "Go to our Web site at www.yourpharmacist.com."

To end the release, use the symbols ### centered at the bottom of the page.

"who, what, when, where, why, and how." The more quickly the editor can assess what you're offering, the more likely he or she is to be interested in your story.

News Release Format

For ease of preparation and ultimate use, every news release should contain similar elements. Here are some of the important components.

Source Information. The source information is the name and phone number of the person whom the media should contact if they want more information. In most situations, your own name or that of a staff member will be appropriate. It should appear in the upper right corner of the page.

Even if you are reproducing the news release on letterhead that contains your phone number elsewhere on the page, be sure to put the phone number with the source information anyway. That's where an editor expects and wants to see it. Be sure the phone number you include is one that is always covered during business hours.

Release Date. Most news releases are labeled "FOR IMMEDIATE RELEASE." This label means that the story can be used as soon as it is received or at the earliest convenience of the media.

If a release does not specify "FOR IMMEDIATE RELEASE," it should specify a date: "FOR RELEASE, MONDAY, NOVEMBER 6," for example. This is acceptable, but it can lessen your chances for coverage. Specifying a particular date means that the media must hold your release for a period of time. In general, the more complicated your news is to handle, the less interested in it the reporters may be.

There are, however, occasions when it is appropriate to withhold the release. Suppose that you are sponsoring a community service awards dinner. You want to get the information about the event out to the media in advance so that people can put it on their calendars; however, you want the publicity to occur just after the event, so that the names of the honorees can be included. In this case, media material announcing the community service award winners could be prepared ahead of time. The information might then be labeled "FOR RELEASE, SATURDAY, JULY 11, 10 P.M."—by which time the dinner should be over and the honorees' names announced. Editors would know that on the Saturday late evening television news, or in the Sunday morning paper, they could report the names of those who had been honored at the dinner.

Headline. The headline of the news release is a straightforward summary of its main content. It is typed in capital letters.

When writing the headline, be sure to put the reader-interest information first: "FREE GLAUCOMA SCREENINGS FOR SENIORS TO BE HELD..." rather than "SMITH'S PHARMACY TO HOLD GLAUCOMA SCREEN-

INGS..." In this case, the important information for the reader (and, therefore, the editor) is what is happening and for whom, not who is sponsoring it.

Catchy headlines are not appropriate on news releases; editors expect a factual summation telling exactly what the story is about.

Dateline. The dateline includes the city and state in which the news release originates. The dateline is particularly helpful when sending a release to newspapers or magazines that cover several regions.

Body of the News Release. News releases should follow the basic format of newspaper stories. This style means that they should be written in a form known as the "inverted pyramid." All vital details are presented at the beginning of the story, and other information appears in descending order of importance.

The reason for this structure is that news stories need to be of flexible length. If space permits, the whole release may run. Otherwise, only the first paragraphs may be used. If the release is written in the inverted pyramid style, the most important information will still be conveyed, even if the release has to be truncated because of insufficient space.

If your release runs more than one page, space it so that you have a full paragraph ending at the bottom of every page and a new paragraph beginning at the top of the next page.

Continued Pages. If your release goes to more than one page, type the word "-more-" at the bottom of each page that leads on to a continuing page of the release. Subsequent pages should be labeled with the page number and release title in the upper left corner: "Page 2 – *Medication Tips*."

News releases that run more than one page should always be stapled to minimize the chance that a page will be lost.

End of the Release. Indicate the end of the release by putting "###" or "END" or "-0-" after the final paragraph.

Writing Style

Keep your sentences and paragraphs short and your wording simple. Avoid glorifying your story. Superlatives like "fantastic," "world's best," and "one-of-a-kind" have no place in a news release unless you have facts to back you up. If you're claiming to be the "first," then be sure you are. If your pharmacy is the "oldest" in the area, provide data to substantiate your claim. Try to be as objective as possible. Let the story speak for itself.

Why such caution? There are two reasons. First, a self-serving release won't sell well to an editor. It's better to pique the editor's curiosity with a factual news release, so that he or she will send a reporter out to cover your story. Then the reporter can say you're wonderful!

The other reason for not glorifying your story is that editors sometimes need copy that they can quickly plug into a blank space on the page. They often take a story and print it word-for-word from the release. If your release gives a glowing description of your business, a newspaper editor—who strives to fill the paper with objective reporting—can't select your release to fill that blank space. He or she may not have time to send a reporter out to see if you're as good as you say you are.

This doesn't mean that you should not make every effort to portray your business in the best-possible light. If you do have good news to report, there are ways to include positive information about yourself. For example, if you have statistics or facts that tell the story, use them. If you're the only pharmacy in your area to have an asthma management program, and if because of this program, patients have been saved from hospitalization, that's a story you have every reason to share.

You can also place information that praises you in quotes—quotes of a satisfied patient, customer, or other healthcare professional. Perhaps, for example, the asthma patient who has taken back control of his life would be willing to be quoted on how great your program is.

You can also quote yourself on more objective subjects such as expansion of service or an increase in business. As long as the release is written so that it does not appear that the newspaper or magazine is saying all those great things about you, your good news can be useful news to the media.

Finally, before sending out your release, be sure to proofread it carefully. Pay particular attention to names, titles, and degrees.

Sending Out the Release

There are several ways to send your news release out. You can mail the release, fax it, or e-mail it to the editor. Check with the editors as to which method they prefer.

Address news releases to the news directors of local radio and television stations. Immediate news, information about an upcoming event, or possible feature story can be telephoned to the news director, assignment editor, or reporter.

Follow up with a letter and, if appropriate, a media kit that includes additional information on the event, your practice, and its efforts. If appropriate, provide a list of experts who can be contacted regarding the story.

Newspapers and news stations put releases to varied uses. If a piece is considered inappropriate for a radio news segment, it may be something disc jockeys can use, such as an event announcement. Or the program director could decide to use it as the basis for a caller participation show, community service show, or talk show. Don't try to tell the stations where or how to use your information. Let them decide.

Sample News Release

FOR IMMEDIATE RELEASE   CONTACT: Media Liaison
Date   (000) 000-0000

PHARMACISTS HELP CONSUMERS USE
MEDICINES SAFELY AND EFFECTIVELY

CITY, STATE – Following the pharmacist's advice can save money for consumers and help lower the nation's healthcare bill by ensuring proper medication use. Not following a medicine's instructions or discontinuing its use without a doctor's advice can lead to a more expensive treatment, such as surgery or hospitalization.

"Today's medicines are more powerful than ever before and have the potential to do a great deal of good," said [YOUR NAME AND AFFILIATION]. "But wonder drugs will only work wonders if they are properly managed. Monitoring the medication use process and advising patients on safe medication practices is the primary role of the pharmacist."

Consumers should patronize pharmacies where pharmacists provide medication-counseling services, including drug regimen reviews and drug interaction checks; coordinate patient care with physicians; and monitor side effects. Some pharmacists also are able to perform limited patient testing, such as cholesterol screens, glucose monitoring, and blood pressure checks, for serious health-threatening problems.

By working together with your pharmacist, you can be sure that your medications are taken safely, effectively, and appropriately to maintain your good health.

###

Media Advisory or Alert

You can use a media advisory or media alert to draw attention to an event that you want the media to attend. The advisory is particularly valuable in soliciting television coverage.

A media advisory begins with a simple "who, what, when, where" format. Details of "why" and "how" are presented in the body of the advisory. Don't forget the visual aspects, that is, what there will be to photograph.

Media advisories can be used in combination with news releases and pitch letters. A media advisory is often sent, faxed, or e-mailed to the media the day before or the day of an event.

A media advisory, followed by a phone call, should provide just enough information to entice reporters to your event. Provide a news release on site, possibly as part of a media kit, with enough details to help the reporters write the story.

A media advisory is not used for advance publicity, which should be handled with a news release sent weeks before the event.

Sample Media Advisory

FOR IMMEDIATE RELEASE   CONTACT: Media Liaison
Date   (000) 000-0000

MEDIA ADVISORY
PHARMACISTS TO CONDUCT
"BROWN BAG" MEDICINE REVIEW

WHAT: A "Brown Bag" Medicine Review will be held in conjunction with National Pharmacy Week, October [DATE]. Pharmacists from [YOUR PHARMACY] have asked the public to bring in their medicines—prescription and nonprescription—for a checkup. Pharmacists will be available for personal consultations to ensure that each person is not using or storing expired medications and is not taking medications, that, when taken together, could cause unwanted side effects.

WHEN: [DATE]
              9 a.m. to 5 p.m.

WHERE: [YOUR PHARMACY]
              [ADDRESS]
              [CITY/STATE]

WHY: Pharmacists will encourage participants to *Talk With Your Pharmacist*. By speaking with their pharmacists about their medicines, patients can ensure healthy results.

            Find out how to store medications safely, what questions to ask about your medicines, and which nonprescription medicines should not be taken with certain prescription medications.

###

Other Types of News Releases

News releases prepared for print media are the most common. However, some events might require use of video or audio news releases. Here's some information that will help you get started.

Video News Releases

Video news releases (VNRs) are releases sent to TV stations. They are produced on broadcast-quality videotape and sent to stations by overnight or first-class mail, depending on the urgency of the message. They can also be transmitted to the stations via satellite. The printed matter enclosed with the tape or sent in advance of a satellite transmission describes briefly what is being sent. VNRs are expensive to produce. They could cost $25,000 or more, including distribution.

There are two basic types of VNRs. The first is used in connection with a newsworthy event such as the announcement of a new product. It is released at the same time as it is announced to the print media. The second type of VNR, "evergreen" stories, are used in situations that do not have an immediate or "hard" news angle.

Research indicates that more than 90% of TV news departments use outside-produced videos as resources for stories. Although complete VNRs are accepted, most news departments edit the story to fit their needs, especially in the nation's top 50 markets. Some stations insert their own voice-overs and identification tags and present the material as if it were produced in-house.

Although VNRs can be effective, they are also regarded with suspicion by some television news directors, who are sensitive to anything that hints of commercialism.

Audio News Releases

Audio news releases are brief statements about an event or story—why it is newsworthy and how it relates to the station's audiences in terms of audience relevance. They are sent to radio stations in place of print releases. They can be sent over a telephone line if the station expresses interest.

A radio release should have the name of a person who can be contacted for further information, plus the offer of a source for an expert's interview (also over the phone).

Radio releases should arrive at the station in advance of a print release that may be sent to the print media. Once the story has appeared in the local newspaper, it is of no value to a radio station.

Feature Articles

Newspaper and magazine editors like stories that have human interest—stories that deal with who people are, what they do, and why they do it. Feature articles are commonly used to expand on a news story, add color or background, or present a particular slant or point of view. Features are designed for special reader appeal and impact. Radio and television stations are less likely than newspapers to use feature stories, as they are not considered hard news.

The success of a feature article is determined by its ability to interest the reader. The theme and angle must be fresh enough to draw interest, and the form of the narration must be interesting. The story must appear in a publication whose readership is interested in the subject that the feature covers.

Although feature stories may not be as time oriented as hard news, most of them do have a certain timeliness. A first guideline to keep in mind, therefore, is that if your story idea relates to a program or an event that has a termination date or a timeliness to it, you must start well in advance and allow ample lead time.

With respect to generating feature stories, you have several choices. The first is to try to interest a reporter in doing a story. Create an outline that contains the main points. Then send or take it to the editor of the first publication on your list. Talk it over and see if he or she will assign a writer to work with you on it. You could also go to a staff writer for the publication and ask him to go to his editor for permission to write the story. You may approach a freelance writer whose work you admire.

The second option is to write the story yourself. If you submit a story to a publication, the editor may ask you to rewrite it to fit certain requirements—perhaps as to length, perhaps as to subject matter. Or the editor may ask you for permission to rewrite it. It is almost always wise to grant this permission, but you should ask to see the finished product before it is printed. It is possible that someone else's rewrite might prove embarrassing to you.

In either event, be aware that a feature article, as opposed to the news story, is submitted to just one publication at a time. Only when your idea has been formally rejected can you take it to the second target publication on your list.

Op-Eds

An op-ed is an article expressing an opinion. Op-eds often appear on the page opposite a newspaper's editorial, hence their name. Most op-eds are about 800 words long (about three double-spaced pages); however, their length may run from 300 to 1200 words, depending on the publication.

Op-eds can be serious, satirical, or light hearted. They can spark a debate, highlight a neglected point of view, and offer a new perspective. Unlike editorials, which are written by news staff, op-ed opinion articles are written by advocates themselves to express a viewpoint. Taking the time to put your opinions in writing demonstrates your concern for the issue or event. For example, you may want to write an op-ed on your observations of a drug education program in your community.

When to Do an Op-Ed

When you, your pharmacy, or local pharmacy association is involved with and has a point to make on a major newsworthy issue (such as trends in health-care), the op-ed page provides you with the chance to illustrate the value of the profession. An op-ed piece is used to persuade readers to adopt or support an organization's viewpoint on an issue. Papers will also, however, occasionally publish a philosophical piece that may comment on a continuing problem, such as medication misuse or an observation on society.

A timely, well-written, and provocative piece in a national publication can establish the writer as an expert on a particular topic and gain widespread media recognition for its author. Newspaper editors and broadcasting producers read the op-ed pages of national newspapers when seeking experts on particular subjects. Op-ed editors also solicit pieces from writers with whom they have established a relationship or from people with expertise on topics in the news.

Editors at large newspapers or magazines receive hundreds of op-eds each week and must weigh several factors when choosing which ones to publish. The criteria include the article's quality, timeliness, freshness of viewpoint, and the number of articles already published on the topic.

Authors of op-eds are often paid a small amount; some papers offer a stipend as high as $350. However, many newspapers offer no compensation but the pride of authorship.

Choosing a Topic for an Op-Ed

Persuasive writing and good credentials are not enough to get an op-ed published. You need a subject that is current and appeals to the audience. An original point of view on a much-talked about issue will also make your piece stand out. You will be more likely to get a newspaper to accept an op-ed if the issue is important to the community.

Be sure you address an issue that involves a real debate; don't argue an obvious position, such as "Crime is bad." Hotly debated issues generally produce many submissions, and editors will select only the best to print. Editors try to cover a variety of issues, so if you have already seen your topics addressed on the editorial page, you are unlikely to get your piece placed there. Select another topic or try another newspaper.

If you must write about a popular issue, factors that may help you get published include pertinent credentials or personal experiences that make you uniquely qualified to write about the subject. A point of view contrary to pre-vailing public opinion or the newspaper's editorial position will also greatly improve your placement chances. Be aware that you may not be the only one to write about an issue and that editors look to balance the subject matter on their pages.

Guidelines for Writing Op-Eds

Op-eds are, first and foremost, designed to express an opinion. Therefore, your piece must make your viewpoint clear. Focus on one idea. Have opening and closing paragraphs that clearly state your conclusion or opinion.

Avoid cliches, jargon, or "legalese." Use simple, straightforward language. Don't use an acronym unless you first spell it out. Express your opinions strongly, but do not be rude or offensive.

Verify all your facts and names. Read your piece over for spelling and grammar. Mistakes can hurt your credibility. Review the piece to be sure it flows well and does not contain leaps in logic.

Stick to the word limits set by the publication. Your piece will be less likely to be selected if it does not fit the format.

End with your name, title, and a phone number.

Type the op-ed double spaced on $8\frac{1}{2} \times 11$-inch paper. Include your name and contact number on each page and a key word alongside the

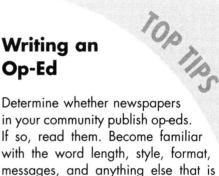

Writing an Op-Ed

Determine whether newspapers in your community publish op-eds. If so, read them. Become familiar with the word length, style, format, messages, and anything else that is distinctive. Incorporate these elements into your op-ed.

Decide on a topic. If appropriate, relate your topic to a current issue. Samples include the role of the pharmacist in the healthcare system and the reasons why pharmacy services have to be an important part of the healthcare agenda.

If the editor shows some interest, do a draft.

Make sure your op-ed is consistent with the format and length of op-ed pieces that generally appear in the publication that you've targeted. Give your draft to a few people for review.

Submit the draft. If you've promised an editor you will have a draft by a certain date, do so.

Remember, an interest in reviewing an op-ed does not necessarily mean the publication will use the piece, even if it is particularly well written. You may have to adapt the op-ed to the editor's wishes or provide back up for points you make in the piece.

page number. Including them will help the reporter in the event the pages become separated from one another.

Submitting the Op-Ed

When submitting an op-ed, be aware that exclusivity is almost always required by the national newspapers and preferred by many local newspapers—although some local papers do allow multiple submissions outside their general circulation area. Check individual newspaper guidelines on this issue. Smaller papers generally accept multiple submissions, as long as competing papers in the same city do not run the same piece. Again, check each publication's particular policy.

In some cases, pitch letters can be effective tools to propose an op-ed column to a publication. Send a pitch letter to appropriate editors outlining the proposed topic and author. If you have established a relationship with a particular editor, make a call. Be prepared to make a quick summary of the main points of your proposed article.

You may also submit the op-ed "cold." In this case, send the op-ed to the largest paper first, unless you are targeting a specific geographic area. If it is rejected, try another, then another. Don't be discouraged if it takes a couple of tries to secure the placement.

In most cases, completed op-eds should be sent by first-class mail. Some newspapers also accept op-eds by fax or e-mail. These methods are especially useful if the piece is timely and could become dated quickly. However, before submitting an op-ed by fax or e-mail, check the newspaper's submission policies.

Many op-ed editors will call to let you know if they plan to use a piece, but few will contact you if they reject your submission. To encourage a response, enclose a self-addressed, stamped envelope with your submission.

Keep phone calls to editors at a minimum and don't call them near the end of the day when they are on deadline. Your piece should stand alone and not need further explanation or interpretation. If the editors can't figure it out, the readers probably won't get it either.

Once you're been published, make photocopies of the column with the newspaper's masthead and date. Send it to people of influence. Include it in your media kit.

Letters to the Editor

One section of the newspaper that is always enjoyable is the Letters to the Editor. A letter is an excellent way to respond to a newspaper when it has run a story or an editorial on an issue of concern to your organization.

A letter to the editor should be short—no more than 400 words. The shorter the letter, the more likely it is to be printed without being edited. Make your most important point in the first paragraph. If your letter

Sample Op-Ed Article   Contact: [Your Name]
                                (000) 000-000

INAPPROPRIATE USE OF PRESCRIBED MEDICATIONS IS AN EMERGING PUBLIC HEALTH CRISIS IN THE U.S.

There is an emerging public health crisis in the United States—the inappropriate use of prescribed medications.

A recent study estimated the cost of the problems caused by inappropriate use of legally prescribed medications to be $76.6 billion. This estimate is the cost created by patients using medications their doctors prescribe, but not in the manner intended. An antibiotic fails to cure an infection because the patient stopped the therapy too soon...a patient with asthma is rushed to the emergency room because he did not understand how to use his inhaler... a grandmother with diabetes slowly loses her eyesight because she has not been trained to test and control her blood glucose levels.

The profession of pharmacy is prepared to accept responsibility for fixing this problem. As the healthcare professional with the most medication-specific training and as the most accessible healthcare professional (particularly in rural areas), the pharmacist can work with patients to improve their use of medications and decrease the costs of drug therapy problems.

Pharmacists are now being trained with a primary focus on patient care, on helping medications work better by educating the patient, and on monitoring drug therapy. Nearly all of the schools and colleges of pharmacy are granting the Doctor of Pharmacy degree for the completion of a four-year professional curriculum. More than 15,000 pharmacists have completed some type of advanced training to improve their patient care skills—and many more pharmacists are planning to develop such skills.

Another study published in the *Journal of the American Pharmaceutical Association* showed that the impact of a pharmacist working with patients is significant. In this study, pharmacists worked with patients to improve their management of high cholesterol levels. Pharmacists and patients met monthly to discuss therapy progress and conduct a test to check cholesterol levels. This information was then provided to the physician to ensure collaboration in the care of the patient. In this model—a model developed and used in community pharmacies across the country—84% of the patients were compliant with their medication therapy. This figure is significant when

-more-

Page 2 – *Health Crisis*   Contact: [Your Name]
                                                     (000) 000-000

compared with other studies, which commonly report that only 40% of patients continue their therapy and that 60% of patients discontinue their therapy within 12 months. The patients working with pharmacists not only continued taking their medication, they took it as recommended by their physician.

I believe this model can be replicated across the country, pharmacists working with patients to make the best use of their medication. Making the concept operational, however, does require incentives. Pharmacists, like any other healthcare professional, simply cannot afford to give away their services. Patients and other payers of healthcare (managed care organizations, Medicare, and Medicaid) must recognize the value of drug therapy management services and compensate for them.

[NAME OF ORGANIZATION] is working diligently on this agenda—preparing pharmacists to take responsibility for this problem, educating payers on the value of these services, and explaining the problem of inappropriate medication use to patients.

We have much work to do, however. The interest of public policy-makers is important to our work, important to addressing this public health crisis. In 1998, the government launched a new federal offensive against air traffic accident deaths, with a goal to bring about an 80% reduction in fatal aviation accidents. Based on 1995 statistics, the program aims to save 140 of the 175 annual fatalities from U.S. airline accidents. When Thomas Moore, senior fellow at George Washington University, notes an estimated 100,000 people die each year due to adverse events caused by medication use, it appears an initiative against this threat is also warranted.

[YOUR NAME/CURRENT PROFESSIONAL POSITION (000) 000-0000]

###

responds to a particular article, editorial, or another letter, refer to the title, date, and author of the original piece in your opening sentence. If appropriate, letters to the editor should be signed by an officer of an organization. Weekly newsmagazines and other media also publish letters to the editor, and you should become familiar with the style of these letters, as well as their length and other considerations, which will enhance the likelihood of your letter being printed.

Op-Eds versus Letters to the Editor

There are several differences between op-eds and letters to the editor. The latter generally respond to something previously published in the paper. Letters to the editor are much shorter than op-eds—a few paragraphs instead of several hundred words. Writers often express a personal viewpoint and may not be writing as experts or as representatives of organizations.

If what you have to say is short or offers another view of the newspaper's coverage of an issue, consider submitting a letter to the editor. Letters to the editor include the writer's name, address, and phone number. Editors will call to authenticate the letter before it is published.

It's best to target your letter to a particular publication rather than to send out copies to a variety of editors. Such letters should be addressed to the Editor or Letters to the Editor Department.

You might gain extra mileage from a letter published in a newspaper by sending a copy of it to trade magazines or other publications that might be interested in the subject or the signer of the letter. Simply attach a note indicating that the letter was sent or was published. In some cases, a rebuttal letter or a letter-writing campaign about a controversial issue can be the subject of a news release, particularly to trade or special-interest publications.

At APhA, we often send copies of our letters to the editor of major publications like *The New York Times, The Washington Post*, or *USA Today* to our pharmacy trade publications with a cover memo indicating that they were submitted. Sometimes it makes no difference if it gets published in the major publication. The fact that it was sent can become an important story to the trade audience.

Public Service Announcements

Public service announcements (PSAs) are brief messages that provide helpful information to the public, solicit support for a particular cause, or offer an organization's free services. They can be in print, audio, or video format. Unlike advertising, PSAs are carried free of charge by publications and radio and television stations to educate an audience and to encourage people to do something such as participate, call, write, or contribute.

Radio and TV stations and networks donate the broadcast airtime for these messages. Some PSAs are presented as the joint effort of the sponsoring organization and the station. For example, a PSA might close with: "This message is brought to you as a public service from the Cumberland Pharmacists Association and Station WXXX."

Public Service Media Campaigns: Where Do They Fit?

Public service campaigns have been used in recent years by health promotion and disease prevention programs. As might be expected, competition for public service time and space is very intense. Although neither radio nor TV stations are required to donate a specific amount of time to PSAs or public affairs programming, stations are obligated (as a condition of licensing) to ascertain and respond to the concerns of the community they serve. There is no such incentive for print media, and major newspapers rarely offer free space.

PSAs have a credibility and persuasiveness that few other forms of media possess. The noncommercial nature of PSAs and the environment in which they are aired, during news and public affairs programming, makes them an extremely effective message conduit.

Although the public sees public service announcements as important, credible, and reliable sources of health and medical information, they are limited in their actual impact. PSAs alone will not cause long-term behavior changes, especially with such ingrained behaviors as smoking, sedentary lifestyles, or poor eating habits. For this reason, communications programs designed to affect behavior use PSAs as one component of an overall communication effort that includes an array of mass media and interpersonal communication activities, such as patient counseling and presentation to high-risk individuals and self-help groups for support and reinforcement.

Within the context of a larger communication program, PSAs are most useful for creating awareness or heightening public sensitivity to a health problem or issue or for reinforcing a newly established behavior. A well-designed PSA can transmit specific information to the public

Creating Your Own Live-Read PSA

TOP TIPS

By following a few simple rules, you can create your own live-read PSA. Send it to your targeted radio station. If it is accepted, the host of the show will read it live on air.

Prepare the PSA on your pharmacy's letterhead.

Type your copy in capital letters, double spaced with wide margins to ensure easy readability.

List the date with the name and telephone number of your media liaison in the top right-hand corner, along with the dates the station is to start and stop the broadcast in the top left-hand corner.

Write your message as you would speak, without using abbreviations.

Use advertising copy style—punchy and sharp.

such as announcing the time and place of a health screening. PSAs also are appropriate for increasing recognition of a health program, generating requests for health information, or recruiting volunteers. Unless campaign messages attract attention, however, they are unlikely to succeed at these objectives.

Print PSAs

Magazines provide public service advertising space. Daily newspapers rarely carry advertisements on a public service basis. They don't have the space. Weekly newspapers are more likely to do so. They, along with penny savers and shoppers' guides, offer the best forums for public service print ads. If you have designed a poster or flyer about a special program or event, it can be easily adapted to serve as a print PSA.

Competition for free space is fierce. You must start working with your local print media early if you are seeking placement for a certain month. When attempting to place a PSA in a newspaper or magazine, get in touch with the publication's community development or public service department. Larger publications may have several departments that cater to specific advertisements, so you may need to contact the advertising division responsible for the health section. Explain your PSA and how its message will benefit readers. If they agree to place the camera-ready column, mail the appropriate slick sheet with an introductory letter reinforcing the value of your message.

Broadcast PSAs

Broadcast PSAs are radio or television commercials, usually from 10 to 60 seconds long, that are aired at no cost to the sponsor. Like print PSAs, they always include a call-to-action statement. Three formats are used for broadcast PSAs: preproduced audiotapes for radio; preproduced videotapes for television; and "live-read" (scripted) PSAs, which are delivered by a station personality.

Radio PSAs are among the most effective uses of radio available. As a media tool, PSAs are often overlooked due to the prevailing view that they are used primarily as a means to issue community events information. However, it is precisely this community-oriented aspect that lends such effectiveness to a public service announcement.

Because stations are under no legal obligation to run PSAs, the decision about which PSAs to air resides entirely with individual stations. As a result, messages must be well produced and well presented. Broadcasters use several criteria for determining which PSAs make the air. For example, the sponsor must be held in high esteem; the message must have a strong relevance to the community; and the message design must be original and thought provoking. The primary criterion for a successful PSA is the quality of the message it conveys. In addition, while stations tend to air both event-specific and general

---

Sample Radio Public Service Announcements (PSAs)

DATE:

START: [DATE]   CONTACT: Media Liaison
STOP: [DATE]   (000) 000-0000

30 Seconds

DO YOU RELY ON NONPRESCRIPTION MEDICINES TO RELIEVE YOUR HEADACHE, FEVER, OR ARTHRITIS? IF SO, YOU'RE NOT ALONE. AMERICANS CONSUME MORE THAN 50 BILLION TABLETS EACH YEAR. WHEN TAKEN AS DIRECTED, THEY'RE SAFE AND EFFECTIVE. BUT THEY'RE STILL SERIOUS MEDICINE.

PHARMACISTS WANT YOU TO KNOW THAT THEY ARE ALWAYS AVAILABLE TO TALK TO YOU ABOUT YOUR MEDICATIONS. SO TALK WITH YOUR PHARMACIST FOR YOUR GOOD HEALTH.

THIS MESSAGE IS BROUGHT TO YOU BY THE NATION'S PHARMACISTS, AND [STATE/LOCAL PHARMACY ASSOCIATION, LOCAL PHARMACY, ETC.].

###

10 Seconds

PHARMACISTS WANT YOU TO KNOW THAT THEY CARE ABOUT YOUR HEALTH. BY WORKING TOGETHER WITH YOUR PHARMACIST, YOU CAN BE SURE THAT YOUR MEDICINES WILL MAKE YOU BETTER WHEN YOU ARE SICK OR HELP KEEP YOU HEALTHY. SO TALK WITH YOUR PHARMACIST FOR YOUR GOOD HEALTH.

###

PSAs, broad topic PSAs tend to be more successful because they can be kept for use on an as-needed basis throughout the year.

Before attempting to place a PSA, determine whom you want to reach with your message. Then identify the media outlet that best serves that particular audience. Once you have determined the media outlets you want to target, contact the head of their community development or public service department to find out the proper procedures for submitting PSAs.

Because of the volume of requests they receive, radio stations cannot air every PSA offered to them. It is therefore imperative to provide stations with PSAs that are in the most user friendly format for their personnel to use. In addition, a subject for which a local angle can be found can greatly enhance its desirability to a public service director.

Send your PSA with a cover letter explaining the value of your message. Call your contact(s) shortly after sending the information to confirm that it was received.

Provide the radio station with each version of your PSA to give the station options for various time slots.

News Conferences and Media Briefings

The purpose of a news conference or media briefing is to notify the media of something significant. You might want to consider holding a news conference if you are seeking to influence an event—a bill that is up for vote in the local, state, or national legislature, for example—or to commemorate a special event. A news conference can also be called if you are releasing the results of a poll or a research project. The unique advantage of a news conference over a news release is that it offers reporters the opportunity to interact with your presenters.

Planning and conducting a successful news conference or media briefing requires a great deal of preparation, and the results can be unpredictable. Most public relations activities can be handled by a news release. However, a news conference or media briefing can be appropriate when a subject or issue requires more than the written word.

Think carefully about the decision to move forward with a news conference. Decide whether the event or activity you have in mind truly merits a news conference. If the answer is yes, move forward.

Choosing the Site

The first step is to select an appropriate site. Your options are many. You can hold a news conference just about anywhere—in front of a building, or even on the sidewalk. Another option is to hold it in a press club or hotel, since either allows for more space and would be better equipped. On some occasions, it is wise to call a conference in a dramatic location, but the location must be part of the message, and you must make arrangements to accommodate the media. (If you're planning for an outdoor news conference, be sure to have an indoor backup in case of rain.)

The two most important things to consider in deciding on a location are:

▶ Is this a convenient site for reporters? and

▶ Does this location say anything about the issue being addressed?

The size and decor of the room are important too. Avoid rooms with mirrors and undraped windows, both of which cause problems for television cameras. The room must be large enough to accommodate all the media and their equipment, including television cameras. The room should have an ample supply of two- and three-prong electrical outlets for cameras, lights, and tape recorders.

Time

To boost media attendance and get better coverage, try to schedule news conferences between 9:00 a.m. and 11:00 a.m., and in the middle of the week (Tuesday, Wednesday, or Thursday).

This schedule allows both the newspapers and television time to edit before the evening editions. Do not hold news conferences on Fridays or weekends, because the story will get lost in the weekend news.

Inviting the Media

Inviting the media entails a series of well-timed, coordinated steps. First, three to four weeks before the event, send a news release noting the time, date, location, and reason for the briefing.

In addition, one or two weeks before the event notify the day-books (see Chapter 3). Associated Press, Reuters, and United Press International provide a daily listing of news conferences and other events of interest to their subscribers. If you call your conference at the last minute, fax or e-mail your information. Inclusion in the daybooks can be vital to the success of your event.

A week before the event, send a media advisory. The media advisory should be faxed or delivered to every media outlet you hope will cover your event.

Follow up with a phone call the afternoon before or morning of the news conference. Ask politely but directly whether they plan to attend.

Holding a News Conference

TOP TIPS

Call a news conference only for something extremely timely, controversial, or news-worthy.

Send a news release two weeks or so before the event. Follow up with a media advisory.

Call the invited media the day before the event to get some idea of who will attend and to remind those who have forgotten.

Schedule your news conference in a location convenient for the media.

Schedule your conference in the midmorning, preferably between 9 a.m. and 11 a.m.

Have a sign-in sheet at the door and someone to ensure that all attendees sign in. Give out background materials at the door.

Have no more than three speakers. Keep their remarks to a minimum, and then open the floor to questions.

Choose the right spokespersons. Prepare them for the difficult questions they may have to answer.

Be prepared for radio and television requirements if you expect electronic coverage.

Try to get a commitment. Be enthusiastic ("You don't want to miss this!"). Journalists have to decide each day which stories are worth covering, so make sure yours is on their list.

A final word on invitees: In addition to reporters, invite friends and interested parties. A big crowd usually draws media attention.

Selecting and Preparing Your Spokespersons

One major cause of a failed news conference or media briefing is that the speakers are not well prepared. Choose your speakers carefully, then prepare them well. Hold a dress rehearsal before the actual conference. Have members of your staff drill the speakers with hard-driving questions. This preparation helps prevent slip-ups while the media are present as well as familiarize the speaker with media tactics.

Spokespersons should not read their remarks if possible. Extemporaneous speaking is always more convincing.

The news conference should be no more than 30 minutes long. Make sure that you allow a good deal of time for questions and answers.

Print Materials and Visual Aids

Visual aids such as charts and posters are important, and if you plan on having TV coverage, they are essential. Be creative. The better visuals you have, the more likely you'll have television coverage. A large crowd also makes for a terrific visual.

Photos, biographies, copies of the speeches, and news releases should be available on site so that the media will have the proper background information on the organization as well as the reason for the news conference. Use visual props for television. Enlarged plans and computer-generated photographs or charts are effective visual aids. Often the electronic media will tape the entire conference and then ask to set up a special interview to focus on a specific aspect of the story.

On-Site Logistics

Post signs to help people find the site. Place a table outside the room or just inside for the media to sign-in. Have someone greet attendees and hand out news releases or media kits.

Provide a lectern with a microphone for speakers and space for reporters' microphones. If the room is very large, reporters may need microphones as well.

Make sure that there are well-spaced electrical outlets.

It is helpful to supply free telephones for the media, as well as extra paper, pens, and other useful materials.

Begin the news conference on time.

Follow-Up

After the news conference, send copies of the news release to reporters who were unable to attend. Continue to update reporters on your project's successes, and provide statistics, if applicable.

Monitor the media following the event.

Save all clippings and get copies of all electronic coverage.

One-on-One Interviews

If there are just a few publications that are most important to you, take the message to them on a one-on-one basis. This technique also helps the editors develop your story angle from their publication's point of view.

Select as the interviewee the person from your organization who can best speak about the issue. Call the editors, suggest an angle for their publication, determine interest, and follow up with a letter asking the editors to call you to arrange the interview. If you don't hear back from them in a couple of weeks, phone again.

Be sure the expert is briefed on each publication you plan to visit and the general areas the questions will cover. You can't ask for a list of questions in

PERSONAL EXAMPLE

Media Briefing Tours

Media briefing tours offer an alternative to a news conference. I have often used them successfully.

For example, instead of trying to bring editors from a dozen pharmacy trade publications and consumer publications together in one place, I once embarked on a whirlwind tour with two or three pharmacy experts to visit the offices of these publications. In two days, we met most of the major pharmacy trade publications in New York. We also scheduled meetings with other national publications, such as *Forbes, New York Times, Woman's Day,* and *Good Housekeeping.*

The interest was more than I had expected. While I had planned an hour with each publication, some of the interviews lasted far longer. Because we prepared our presentations well, we were able to generate a number of in-depth articles. Our bonus was making some very valuable editorial contacts and promise of future coverage.

advance, but if you know the publications, how they treat stories or profiles, and the editors, you should know the kind of questions that will be asked and be able to answer them.

Take notes during the interview because someone in your organization will want a report on the meetings. It will also help you recount the meeting if anything appears in print that someone takes issue with.

If the interviewer gets into a sensitive area, be prepared to interject yourself. It's better that you—since you are not being interviewed—take on this role than risk that the interviewee will be forced to say "No comment." Simply point out that the information is proprietary and can't be discussed.

Teleconferences

A teleconference uses satellite technology to beam a news conference to selected sites across the country. Editors are invited just as they are for a traditional media event, and those who are not in the host city (most often New York) watch the event on television as it is transmitted via satellite. The picture transmission is one way, but the audio can go both ways. If the audio is two ways, attendees can engage in the exchange; a reporter in Omaha, for example, can ask a question of someone in a studio in Washington. If the audio transmission is one way, the journalists simply listen and watch.

If you want to reach media in several cities at the same time, a teleconference is a good idea. These events, however, take much preparation and accurate timing, because you must rent satellite time and may have to schedule your event in several different time zones. Your expenses will include receiving equipment in each city (either a studio that has satellite capabilities or rental equipment set up at a hotel or other site). You also must hire technicians to operate the equipment and have your own staff in the various cities to take care of all the arrangements that go with any news conference.

A way to reduce satellite costs is to rent a television studio in each city. Many local stations have this satellite transmission capability. On the other hand, most television studios aren't very fancy, and are not good places to use if food will be served. You will have to have it catered, and even then there may not be enough room in the studio to serve it. In addition, many television studios are not in midtown locations. The size and nature of the audience often will dictate the setting, just as it does for print media events.

Summary

The tools of media communication—news releases, feature articles, news conferences, and others—are well-established and effective. By using them skillfully, you can increase the chance that your public relations program will achieve its objectives.▶

CHAPTER 5

Media Interviews

The phone rings. It's a reporter. She's on deadline and wants to interview you on the spot about recent reports on medication errors and what pharmacists are doing to prevent them. Meanwhile, it's flu season. The pharmacy is backlogged with dozens of unfilled prescription orders, and one-third of your staff is out on sick leave. What do you do?

A s pharmacy gains greater visibility through its activities and the positions that it takes on various matters of public interest, exposure to journalists becomes inevitable. Too often, we tend to view such face-to-face meetings with anxiety, when they should be regarded as opportunities to project a positive impression of the profession and its contributions to patient care.

This chapter provides guidance on how to prepare for an interview and how to interact with reporters during interviews. It emphasizes the need to gain control of an interview in any format—print, radio, or television—and to use the experience as an opportunity to get your important points across.

What to Do When the Media Call

A request for a media interview may be prompted by a breaking news story involving a medication-related issue such as a drug recall. It may also occur if a writer is working on a feature story about healthcare or the pharmacy profession. Regardless of the event or situation that has precipitated the request, show your professionalism by responding in the following manner.

Evaluate the Inquiry

Write down the reporter's name and the name of the publication or broadcast affiliate he or she represents. Ask the specific reason for the interview and how much time will be needed.

Try to determine how knowledgeable the reporter is. Some reporters are extremely knowledgeable about health and business issues. You may occasionally encounter a reporter new to the subject, for example, when the health reporter is

PERSONAL EXAMPLE

Expect the Unexpected

During a pharmacy meeting in Orlando, I received a call from one of the local television affiliates asking if I could provide an interview with a pharmacist about expiration dates on medications. It seemed like a simple request. I located a pharmacist who was attending the meeting who could address this issue. I briefed him on what the reporter had told me would be his story angle.

When the interview began, it seemed like it would be fairly routine. The reporter asked questions such as, "What is the purpose of the expiration date on medicine?" "What happens if someone takes a medication that has expired?"

Just as the pharmacist was beginning to relax and settle into the interview, the reporter pulled out several bottles of over-the-counter medications, including children's products, and shoved them under the pharmacist's nose as the camera was rolling. The reporter then said, "We purchased these children's medications at [name] pharmacy. As you can see, they deliberately placed their bar code labels directly over the expiration dates. When we removed the bar code label, we found that all of these medicines had expired—by a year or so! What do you think of this practice? Is the public in danger?"

Fortunately, the pharmacist had worked with the media before and was able to salvage the situation very adroitly. He explained that those labels were probably placed on the boxes by someone who was stocking the shelves, not by the pharmacist.

The story eventually ran as a three-part series in May (a "sweeps" month!). While the reporter achieved his goal of creating a sensational story, it did not seem as if pharmacists were knowingly trying to sell outdated medications to the public.

If the pharmacist had become rattled or defensive, or responded by indicating that something illegal or immoral had occurred, those would have been the sound bites that appeared in the piece. Instead, the pharmacist came across as the "voice of reason," who explained how this might have occurred.

That's why you can never be too prepared for a media interview, especially before the television "sweeps" periods.

unavailable and someone from another department is assigned. It may also occur if the reporter is working for a small media outlet and must wear many hats.

Ask the reporter how he or she plans to use the interview. Possibilities include strictly as background, as part of a general article or story on the subject in which persons from other professions will also be quoted, or as the basis for an entire story.

You'll find that some interview requests are very straightforward, and it's best not to make them more complicated than they are. Most phone interviews, for example, will fall into one of the following categories:

Fact Check—The reporter needs to verify information from other sources or the interviewer needs additional data.

Round Up—The reporter is calling you, along with others, for comments on an issue or a problem.

Quick Quote—The reporter wants a statement for use in a breaking story.

If the interview falls into one of these categories and you feel comfortable responding, go ahead and do so. Make it clear that you are speaking on your own behalf and not on behalf of your organization.

If you are not comfortable responding immediately, you may want to probe. What is the reporter looking for? Bring the lines of questioning into focus by asking some questions of your own. Ask the reporter about the concept of the story. Who else has been contacted? What other information will be used? How will your information be used? How big will the story be? What is the deadline?

Although your instinct may be to cooperate with the reporter in order to get some publicity, don't feel obligated to give an answer on the spot. Ask what the deadline is and offer to return the reporter's call within a satisfactory time period. The extra time and effort will benefit both sides.

Jot down your key points on the issue before calling back. Return the call as promptly as possible.

Preparing for Media Interviews

TOP TIPS

Know the medium—TV, radio, or print—and the unique requirements of each.

Familiarize yourself with the reporter's background and style.

Be aware of any breaking news stories that may tie into what you may be asked to discuss.

Prepare several points you'd like to make during the interview. Use people-oriented examples to illustrate them.

For interviews by phone, ask whether you are being tape recorded. Always act as though you are being recorded.

Prepare

Except in the case of a breaking news story, there is usually sufficient time between the request and the interview for proper preparation. In instances where the interview has been arranged by a public relations representative, there is almost always time to prepare.

Before an interview for a magazine or newspaper, obtain several recent issues of the publication. Read them carefully to determine how they have handled similar stories. Determine the type of reader for whom they have been written. Keep this imaginary reader in mind when the interview day arrives and tailor your language and use of examples to that reader.

Try to determine the interviewer's position on the topic. This analysis might provide an opportunity to sway the story. In addition, familiarize yourself with the type of stories the interviewer has written by obtaining issues in which he or she has published stories. The fact that you are familiar with his or her work will be flattering and will help establish a good relationship.

Then, using the information you have collected during your initial interview with the reporter, draw up a list of the questions you think might be asked. Work with your colleagues to prepare the answers and practice answering them. If there is time, you could supply a list of questions to the reporter. Be aware, however, that the reporter may not use your questions.

Determine the major points you would like to see in the published article and how you will present them. Be succinct: If you're doing a TV interview, you may appear on the screen for only 20 seconds! Outline your main points on a sheet of paper and take the outline with you to the interview.

There is a good chance that you can give the reporter some supplementary material that will provide greater insight into or understanding of the subject. Prepare such materials in advance, refer to them during the interview, and offer them to the reporter during the interview.

Preinterview Review

Spend time rehearsing with your colleagues your answers to questions you believe will be asked. Have them anticipate questions that the reporter might ask, and prepare your responses. Properly conducted, such a review will uncover gaps in information, missing documents, and uncertainties as to the approach to take. It will reinforce your familiarity with the subject matter, give you direction on how to express yourself best, and alert you to potential trouble areas to be avoided.

Conducting the Interview

If you've never done an interview, don't assume that every reporter has a confrontational, Mike Wallace-type demeanor. The reporter's objective is neither to damage you nor to flatter you. It is to get a good story. Good reporters also pride themselves on accuracy: they want to understand what you have to say as much as you want to say it. To make things go smoothly, try to follow these suggestions.

Interview Site

Arrange a face-to-face interview, rather than a phone interview, if possible. Personal contact is the best means of communication. Eye contact and the ability to read the reporter's body language help you make sure your message is getting across. Once you've established a relationship with a reporter, however, phone interviews may be effective.

In addition, try to have the interview conducted on your home ground—perhaps in an office or conference room. Avoid distractions. Hold your telephone calls, close the door, and minimize interruptions.

Handling the Questions

Provide as much perspective, context, and background as needed to ensure that the reporter has the "big picture." The more information reporters understand, the more accurate the story will be. As noted earlier, it helps to send written materials to the reporter in advance.

Even though a reporter may be rushing you for an answer, take time. Think carefully before you respond. Once the words leave your lips, they are in the control of the reporter and editors. You never can be sure how they will appear in print or on the air, but you can take steps to maximize the chances that they will appear accurately and in context. Try to help focus the reporter's attention on the points you want to make.

Be clear, concise, and thorough. (The drawback of this, however, is that if you are not brief, your response will be edited, and this may distort the meaning.) If it is a sensitive subject that can damage your practice, answer only the questions you are asked. Think before you answer.

Don't be fooled by a reporter's silence. Sometimes reporters remain silent at the end of your remarks, hoping you will continue, possibly stumbling into information you'd just as soon not share. In addition, don't let a reporter put words into your mouth unless you agree with them. Don't repeat the reporter's terminology; your quote is then in effect the reporter's quote.

When speaking in an official capacity, it is best not to give personal opinions. If you decide to do so, be sure the reporter understands that you are speaking for yourself and not for your colleagues.

If you consider a question to be inappropriate, you don't have to answer it.

Finally, never be critical of competitors. You should be interested in projecting your own expertise, not in demeaning others.

Risks of Speaking "Off the Record"

Avoid saying anything you don't want to see or hear on the evening news or read in the newspaper. In other words, never make off-the-record remarks. It's too risky. If you do go off the record, be sure to preface each such statement by saying, "The following material is 'off the record.'" Indicate clearly when your comments are "on the record" again. Do not say belatedly, "The material I have just given is 'off the record.'" It is generally not wise to comment on a controversial issue with the promise that your identity will remain anonymous.

Speaking off the record will not ensure that the statement will not be used. If the reporter goes to the trouble of getting the same information from another source, after you have provided the lead by being off the record, the reporter will be ethically able to use it.

Assume everything you say is on the record and can be used in a news story. If you don't want to read it in the morning, don't share information "in confidence" with a reporter, and don't repeat negative or hostile questions. If you do, they could show up in print next to your name—as a statement instead of a question.

Developing Transitions

If you want to control an interview, you need to develop and practice transitions that will make this possible. For example, to skillfully change the topic, try some of the following tactics.

Changing the Subject

"You mentioned [whatever will tie into your point] before, and it reminds me..."

"That reminds me..."

"Have you ever found yourself in this situation, Dan? You're in your local pharmacy and suddenly..."

"One thing you should know about..."

Contradicting the Reporter's Statement

Don't feel that you have to accept a reporter's facts or figures. If you disagree, say so gracefully and why. If you're not sure, you

---

Responding to Inquiries: A Matter of 1, 2, 3!

Try to follow a formula when responding to each query. The formula consists of three parts: (1) answer the question, (2) bridge to your own positive point, and (3) end with a colorful story or statement. (Remember, *Acknowledge—Bridge—Make a Positive Point*.) Your stories can be word pictures, eye-opening statistics, quotations, anecdotes, examples, metaphors, similes, and comparisons. Use humor with extreme care, especially when talking about people's health.

might say, "That doesn't seem right to me," and ask for time to check the data yourself. Make sure you get back to the reporter with the answer.

Polite Evasiveness

If asked a question you'd rather not handle at the moment, you don't have to answer it. Try one of these techniques.

"Too soon to tell..."

"That's in the future. What I want to talk about now is..."

"What I think you want to know is..."

"Those were important factors, but..."

If asked a question on a sensitive topic, don't be afraid to say, "I can't respond to that."

Above all, never guess and never be afraid to say, "I don't know the answer." Simply tell the reporter that you'll have to check with those who do know the answer and get back to her. Then respond promptly.

Buying Time

Also mentally prepare a list of phrases to use to buy time to think during the interview.

"Well, I thought someone might ask me that..."

"I'm glad you asked that question. Let me take a minute to explain..."

"This is a problem we are studying and expect to soon have..."

Diversionary Tactics

Also have some phrases ready that will enable you to skillfully divert the reporter to the area where you want to focus. These phrases might include the following:

"I don't know...but I happen to believe..."

"That's because..."

"As you know..."

"But perhaps an equally important issue here is..."

"What I think you're getting at is..."

"That's not in my field, but what I can say is..."

Be Audience Oriented

One of the best ways to improve your interviewing skills is to approach the event from the audience's point of view. Will your information improve their health? Save them money? They may be curious about what you've discovered and how you've reached your conclusions, but their primary concern is "What does this do for me?"

In preparing for an interview about a research project, for example, you might want to frame your comments in a way that will answer the following questions:

▶ What is the purpose of your work?

▶ What makes it unusual or unique?

▶ Who will benefit from your research? What would you say is the single most important result of the study or research?

▶ What interested you in this area of study? Why is it important?

Prepare and mentally assemble supporting material: facts, personal experience, contrast and comparison, analogy, definition, statistics, and examples. Keep your responses colorful since reporters are looking for the unusual and dramatic quotes. Personalize your responses and reduce facts and figures to people. Use examples whenever you can to illustrate your point. They not only enliven the story but will often influence an editor to give a story much more prominence than otherwise. If possible, prepare an example involving one person; it's much more effective than dealing with large, anonymous groups of people.

Concluding the Interview

Be sure to summarize your position. At the end of the interview, restate your key points and clarify your message. If you have promised additional information, provide it as soon as possible. Such information might include printed material or the names and phone numbers of other possible interview sources.

If you are concerned about being misquoted, let the reporter know that you would like to tape-record the interview. Be sure to place the recorder where the reporter can see it. If the interview is coming to an end and you have not made an important point, be bold and tell the reporter you would like to make one last point, and do it.

Ask the reporter a question or two near the end of the interview. You may be able to tell from the answers whether your remarks were understood.

Don't ask to read a print reporter's copy, but do offer to answer follow-up questions.

In extremely rare cases, if it appears that the reporter's lack of understanding would result in a grossly inaccurate story, it may be necessary to terminate the interview. In that case, it should be done as gracefully as possible.

If the reporter or you make a serious mistake in a story that has already been published or aired, contact the news outlet and request that steps be taken to have the information corrected.

Postinterview Analysis

Each interview can be a learning experience if you take a few moments afterwards to analyze how it went. Ask yourself the following questions:

Did I convey all of the major points I'd planned?

Were my responses effective? Did I say too little? Ramble too much?

Did I follow through on promises to send the interviewer supplementary materials or get back with answers to questions I didn't respond to on the spot?

Difficult Interviewing Situations

Several problems can develop during an interview. Here are some things that can go awry and some suggestions for overcoming them.

The Hostile Interviewer

Most interviewers want to put you at ease and help you do your best. Unfortunately, some reporters are difficult; they may even pride themselves on their bristly reputation. If you are confronted by a hostile interviewer, stay positive. You don't have to answer a negative question with a negative response.

Never get defensive or appear angry if you are asked a negative question. Rather, take control of the interview. Think of it as a discussion, not an interrogation. Stay calm. Your goal is to make your points whether the interviewer asks you about them or not.

Here are some examples of stereotypical "bad guys" that may make an interview turn hostile and guidelines on how to handle them.

The interviewer who tries to put words into your mouth. After you answer a question, the reporter says "You mean to say that..." Your response should be "No, that is not what I said. What I said was..." then repeat your statement.

The interviewer who launches another three questions before you have begun answering the first one. Stop and tell the interviewer that you will answer the questions—one at a time. Then pick the question that is most positive and answer it first.

The interviewer who constantly interrupts your statements and tries to throw you off your main point. Let the interviewer finish the question, say that you will address it shortly, and go on with the point you were trying to make before the interruption.

The interviewer who tries to pin negative labels on you or phrases questions in such a way as to present a poor image of the profession (for example, "Why isn't pharmacy doing anything to help the elderly with their medications?") Do not repeat the negative, do not become defensive, and do not lose your

PERSONAL EXAMPLE

Stay Calm

One of my former clients, a national medical specialty association, holds an annual meeting where physicians present the results of their research. Two months before one of these meetings was to take place, a national uproar erupted when *The Chicago Tribune* reported that a physician who participated in one study had fabricated patient data. The past president of the association was the lead researcher in charge of this study.

Because the meeting attracted almost 100 journalists—both print and electronic—from around the country, we feared that this negative story might overshadow the meeting. We developed a crisis strategy.

During the meeting, a reporter from a national news magazine appeared with a camera crew and asked to interview the past president on the clinical trial results. A physician, who was the chairman of the association's public relations committee, became involved in a discussion with this reporter. The reporter made an off-hand remark that provoked the physician.

The situation quickly escalated. I attempted to disengage the physician, but he was reluctant to leave. Meanwhile, the camera was rolling. The physician was unaware of this until it was too late. Had this event been featured on the weekly news magazine, it would have made both the PR chair and the association look foolish.

I took the reporter aside and asked him if we could discuss the matter off camera and he agreed. Another member of our PR team escorted the physician back to the meeting.

The reporter agreed not to use film footage of the argument with the physician if we could arrange for a short interview with the association's past president regarding the study. We agreed, and the reporter was satisfied.

It is critical to remain calm when dealing with the media. Remember, they always have the last word.

composure and say, "Hey, that's not a fair question!" You will play into the interviewer's hands and may discredit yourself or your profession. Be positive. Turn the question around. "One of pharmacy's goals is to provide accessible, affordable healthcare for the elderly."

Responding to a Crisis

Once you get known by the media and they trust you, you may be called upon often to comment on stories of interest. From time to time, your advice may be sought in response to a controversial, fast-breaking story.

If a newspaper reporter who knows you calls before the story breaks to get your side of it, you should, of course, think carefully before you answer. But at the same time, those experienced in situations of this kind know that it's better to simply state the facts, never deal in personalities, and try not to be defensive. Controversy on even the most routine subject is more newsworthy than straightforward reporting on noncontroversial news of greater importance. Reporters seem to have an instinctive tendency to ask the kinds of questions that breed and inflame the controversy. With that thought in mind, think carefully.

If you find yourself in such a situation and have no opportunity to present your side before the story appears in print, your best tactic is to calmly call the editor and ask for an opportunity to present your side. This situation may require a letter to the editor, which should be carefully prepared.

Dealing with Errors

Editors and reporters pride themselves on objectivity and accuracy, but sometimes errors that may upset you and your associates can creep into stories. This is equally true for a story that has originated in an interview as for one that is based on the reporter's research.

In such a situation, you have several options.

The first is to do nothing. Try to look at the error objectively. Is it simply a minor misrepresentation? Or is it something that could seriously damage your own reputation or mislead consumers?

If the error is minor but does merit comment, you might mention it in passing to the editor if the opportunity arises. You might also want to determine whether it was indeed an error, an expression of an editor's opinion, or information obtained from another source. It's possible the trouble can be traced to not providing the editor with enough information in the first place or not providing additional information when requested.

If the error is somewhat serious, a polite letter is in order. You may precede this with a phone call to the editor that brings the error to his or her attention and indicates that the letter will spell out your points in more detail. Don't ask that it be run in the letters to the editor column (although it might very well be).

TOP TIPS

Controlling the Interview

Remember that the interviewer needs you for the story.

Create rapport by using the interviewer's first name and maintaining eye contact.

Use gestures to add visual interest.

Listen to the whole question before responding.

Have your key points ready, and use them. Stay within your area of expertise.

Anticipate difficult questions and rehearse answers to them.

Don't discuss anything you do not want used on the air or in print.

Use examples to gain additional talk time.

Speak at your own pace.

Correct significant errors or misstatements at once, tactfully.

Never say something "off the record."

Turn a negative question into a positive answer.

Never lose your temper or argue with a reporter.

If the problem is more serious, write a letter and ask that it be used in the letters column to set the record straight. You need to have all the facts to back up your statement, but keep the letter short. Letters to the editor seldom run more than three or four paragraphs and editors have the right to edit them.

If the error is very serious, ask for a formal correction. Normally, in this situation, a statement of the error is followed by the correction. Be warned, though, that the editor might follow this statement with a critical one of his or her own.

Regardless of the degree of seriousness, never threaten legal action. Don't have your letter signed by a lawyer. You may, however, want to have it reviewed by a lawyer to make sure your facts are straight and you are not putting your practice in an untenable position.

Special Strategies for Radio and TV Interviews

Most of the comments made in this chapter apply to any interview situation. This section contains some special advice concerning radio and TV interviews.

Differences between Print and Broadcast Media

Today, newspapers are no longer the prime source of news for most Americans. It is television. Thus, broadcast media—what *Broadcasting* magazine calls "the fifth estate"—are growing more critical as a publicity outlet, especially with the proliferation of cable television and satellite program transmission. Meanwhile, radio has held its own as a viable publicity outlet.

The public's increasing appetite for visually exciting news is reflected in the growth of local news shows. Many shows that used to be on for a half-hour at dinnertime and again at 11:00 p.m. are now broadcasting in the morning, midday, an hour or more at preprime time, and again at 11:00 p.m. The audience is there not only for the local shows but for cable as well. Interview and talk shows, as well as health and business news, are also popular offerings.

Working with the broadcast media requires some special skills and approaches. You must understand the requirements of news directors or program producers, just as you understand the requirements of print editors. You must also be familiar with how these media work. The news that interests a radio or TV reporter is often different from that directed to print.

First, unlike print, broadcast is not a "targeted" medium. In general, television is directed to vast numbers of people. Thus, any publicity material released should be of fairly wide interest. Moreover, unlike print, broadcast gives far less time to tell your story. Broadcast stories are here and gone in just a few seconds. So you must be aware when recommending or creating publicity material for broadcast that the best you can expect is increased awareness and a favorable impression.

Unlike print, broadcast is a costly medium. Because it is highly visual, the cost of a video news release can run to thousands of dollars, compared with only a few hundred for a print release. Furthermore, broadcast's effects are difficult to measure. And the results of the publicity efforts are harder and more expensive to merchandise than those from the print media. Unless the program is transcribed, there is no permanent record—as there is for print—to show for your efforts.

Television and radio publicity work best when they're part of a well-organized program, but they should not be the focal point. Develop a well-planned, strategic approach using all the appropriate media. Unless you understand how broadcast works and use it wisely, your effort and investment will be wasted.

Interview Strategies for Broadcast Media

Usually, you will have 15–20 seconds to respond to a reporter's question during a radio or television interview. You must be able to relate the entire message in very short sentences and in an interesting and appealing way. Use simple words and avoid jargon and technical terms whenever possible. Long sentences and complex concepts increase the chance that you will be misquoted.

Live versus Taped Interviews

Because reporters often need to respond immediately to breaking news, much of their work is done over the telephone. A reporter may be gathering information for an in-depth story or just looking for a brief comment. Summarize your position and be prepared to answer specific questions.

Broadcast media interviews may be live or taped. Determine the situation at the outset. Remember that you can decline to be aired live or taped and still cooperate with the reporter by providing the information needed for the story.

In an interview that will be edited, you should make your point first—clearly and concisely. Then you can go on to enlarge the point with background. This approach lessens the chances of having your remarks edited out of context.

Take your time and start again if your answer gets jumbled or confused. Don't hesitate to say, "I'd like to try that again."

Studio Interviews

Studio interviews are used for live talk shows, which sometimes have listener call-in options. They may also be used for community service programs. Keep in mind that listeners cannot see you or any gesture you may use to explain or emphasize your point. Keep sentences short and easy to understand. Deliver your message as clearly as possible.

Be poised, speak clearly, and keep eye contact with the reporter. Shifting or glancing about distracts viewers from what you are saying. Don't lean into the microphone; let the reporter position it. If you gesture, do so slowly and with purpose.

Television gives you the option of using slides or videotape to illustrate your points, relevant data, or anticipated results. Preview your slides or video prior to the date of your interview. Also, let the interviewer know that you plan to use visuals. The interviewer or production staff may want to preview your materials for format and quality or to determine how best to use them.

How to Prepare for and Act during a TV Interview

If the interview is to be held in your office or practice site, schedule a location that is not only visual but also complements your point of view. Consider and arrange the background. Look for props or visual examples. Avoid backgrounds that look shabby, cluttered, or outdated.

If the interview is to take place at a TV station, arrive at the television studio early to become familiar with surroundings. Check the chair or sofa they offer you for comfort. Sit on the front part of the chair, lean slightly forward to show your involvement. Plant your feet firmly on the ground and do not cross your legs. Eat lightly before the interview, and avoid anything that is too hot or too cold. Heat expands the vocal cords and makes your voice husky. Cold constricts them and causes other problems. Milk or cream tends to thicken the voice and make you sound as though you need to clear your throat.

Clothing and Makeup

Your wardrobe should be simple and tasteful. Dress in soft, medium, or pastel colors. Avoid very dark or light clothing and contrasting patterns and stripes. Women should not wear noisy bracelets, bright, sparkling jewelry, or overwhelming scarves. Dull finishes, like pearls, are best. Don't wear sunglasses or photosensitive glasses. Don't wear red or white socks and be sure your socks are long enough to cover the calf if you cross your legs.

Men should wear makeup if they have a dark beard, a tendency toward 5 o'clock shadow, a high forehead, or a receding hairline. Brushing your face with cornsilk or translucent pressed powder helps reduce shine and perspiration. Paper (not tissue) also helps absorb oil.

Routine street makeup is adequate for women. Avoid dark or heavy lipstick. Avoid eye shadow that is too bright or that shimmers.

The Microphone

Maintain a distance of 6–8 inches from the microphone and talk normally.

Talk over your lavaliere microphone. If the interviewer is on the right, have the mike pinned on the right-hand side of your shirt or blouse.

Before the interview, a technician will ask you to speak into the microphone to set audio levels. On this audio check, make sure you are speaking at your usual voice level.

Radio and Television Interviews

TOP TIPS

Be prepared. You will be more confident and comfortable, and be able to tell your story clearly to those who count most—the viewers or listeners.

Before the interview, make sure you and the reporter agree on the topics to be covered. Give the reporter a list of the questions you would like to be asked. Be prepared to answer them. If you're doing a radio interview, you may jot down some ideas on file cards.

Be early, even if the interview is to be taped rather than live. Studios are heavily booked, so punctuality is essential.

Make your responses colorful and short. Ten to 25 seconds may well be the entire interview that airs. Practice beforehand and time your answers. You will be surprised how much you can say in such a short time if you are prepared.

If the interviewer asks a negative question, rephrase it positively; do not repeat it.

If the question contains incorrect information, correct it. Don't let the reporter move on until you are confident the point has been cleared.

How to Act

Smile. TV accentuates good and bad facial features. To loosen up your face, concentrate on your forehead. If you have a mustache, you need to invest extra effort in facial gestures.

Sit upright and on the edge of your seat. This position helps emphasize not only enthusiasm but also the best posture. If you sit back comfortably, you will look like you are slouching.

If you must, cross your legs away from the camera. Look at the interviewer, not the camera, unless doing a remote broadcast. Don't shift your eyes, even during questioning.

If standing, avoid movement. One technique is to point one foot forward and put your weight on that foot, leaning toward the mike. You will look like you are interested in the discussion and will avoid bobbing, weaving, or other movement.

Practice hand control. Stick to a few, practiced gestures. Otherwise, keep your hands at your side. Curb habits such as checking your watch, rubbing your hands together, and so forth.

PERSONAL EXAMPLE

Be Prepared

I was working with a television producer on a story about potentially fatal medication errors that occurred in a pharmacy. I selected a pharmacist expert to be interviewed on the subject, and we scheduled a date and time for the taping.

On the appointed day, the producer had another story to cover so she sent her assistant producer to conduct the interview. Although she gave the assistant producer a set of questions she wanted answered, this person did not have any background in this area. The pharmacist being interviewed was able to direct the questions to the points we had wanted to make because the interviewer did not have enough background on the subject to ask further in-depth questions that might have been off the message we wanted to get across.

However, even if the interview had been conducted by the producer who had spent a good deal of time researching this story, the pharmacist was prepared with three points she was going to make during the interview anyway. As it turned out, the pharmacist made the points in a possibly less hostile environment.

Remember that a TV reporter is doing an interview whether the camera is on or not. Any statement made in the presence of the reporter or photographer is fair game. You are never off the record simply because the camera is off.

Radio Call-In Shows

Radio call-in shows are popular. Their informality lends itself well to an interchange of valuable information. In this medium, you must rely on the sound of your voice to emphasize key points.

The guidelines that apply to print interviews should be followed with broadcast media. But the added dimension of voice quality requires attention to a few more points.

Show your enthusiasm by talking with animation—varying your pitch, volume, and rate of speaking.

Create visual imagery by using anecdotes and descriptive phrases. Don't say, "The legislation could have some overall bad effects." Rather explain that, "If this bill is passed, the poor in our community will lose all benefits, middle class workers will be short-changed, and ultimately the costs of healthcare could rise."

Be diplomatic. The people who call in to talk shows remain anonymous. Unfortunately, this means that they may occasionally become aggressive and rude. Maintain your composure. Remember, you're talking to the listening audience, not the caller, so respond to their need to know. Keep in mind that the audience also can spot a rude caller and will weigh credibility appropriately. If your composure starts to slip, suggest that the moderator move on to the next call.

CASE STUDY: Crisis Management

We learned that *Dateline NBC* was working on an investigative report about pharmacists involved in dispensing medications with a potentially dangerous drug interaction. The segment was scheduled to be aired in six weeks.

We contacted the producers to offer them background information on the subject and to make pharmacist spokespersons available to them for interviews. We learned that the program described an investigation involving 11 pharmacies in five states that found that 30% of pharmacy personnel dispensed a dangerous drug combination (cisapride and erythromycin) to consumers with no accompanying warning of the potentially fatal drug interactions represented by this combination.

There were four outcomes from the visits to these pharmacies: (1) pharmacists refused to fill the prescription orders because of the potential drug interaction; (2) pharmacists filled the prescription orders but warned the patient not to take the two medications together; (3) pharmacists filled the prescription orders and provided no warning when the prescription was picked up, but later called the patient to provide a warning; or (4) pharmacists filled the prescription order and provided no warning.

A pharmacist selected from the APhA leadership agreed to participate in a taped interview in response to the findings of this report. The pharmacist went to New York, where he was interviewed for 2½ hours by the program's health correspondent. However, when it aired, the total segment was edited to 10 minutes, and the pharmacist's interview was cut to little more than one minute. The portions of the spokesperson's interview that were actually used were, of course, at the discretion of the producer. (Appendix C provides some guidelines for APhA spokespersons.)

Talking Points

In preparation for the airing of the program, APhA issued talking points to its leadership and its state affiliates and made the information available for any pharmacist who might be contacted by local media for a comment. The points were as follows:

▶ Do not deny the findings of this random survey. Acknowledge that there are system problems which pharmacists are working to solve.

▶ Reinforce that it is the pharmacist's responsibility to identify and prevent dangerous drug interactions.

Core Issues

We also created a set of core issues that should be stressed during any response. These issues were as follows:

▶ Pharmacists are the drug experts and have the responsibility to screen for and warn patients about drug interactions. Pharmacists are uniquely positioned to help patients use their medications most effectively and safely.

▶ Patients and pharmacists are natural allies in this new managed care environment. Patients must form strong relationships with their pharmacists. They must choose their pharmacist carefully.

▶ Medications are powerful and are being used more aggressively in today's healthcare environment. When used correctly, they can help patients recover more quickly; when used incorrectly, they can be harmful.

Questions and Answers

In addition, APhA prepared a list of questions that might be anticipated and model responses to them. The questions and answers were as follows:

Why did the pharmacist call back later? Is this acceptable? It is acceptable. The pharmacist could have realized that the patient got out of the pharmacy before the pharmacist had a chance to talk with her/him (very easy in a busy store). A warning was provided; however, it would have been preferable for the pharmacist to counsel the patient on site.

How did the pharmacist let the patient leave? Aren't there laws requiring pharmacists to counsel patients? There are significant differences in state practice acts regarding the mandatory counseling of patients. However, the pharmacist in this situation had a responsibility to warn the patient of this potential drug interaction. In most cases, the pharmacy is required to offer to counsel the patients. In some states, this offer must be made verbally; in others, a posted sign on the wall offering to counsel or providing written information on the medication fulfills the legal requirement.

What would have happened to a patient who took one dose of these medications? Would the patient have died? The death of a patient because of this particular drug interaction would be very rare. This interaction occurs with patients who take a higher than normal dose of cisapride, and it takes time for the concentration of the drug to build to the level in the body that would trigger this interaction. Pharmacists rely on their professional training, experience, and knowledge to make clinical judgments in various circumstances based on the individual patient.

Can you explain why 30% of pharmacists did not warn patients about a potential deadly drug interaction? I can't speak for the specific pharmacists in this case, although I can say that failing to warn patients about potentially deadly drug interactions is not an acceptable standard of pharmacy practice. I am not attempting to make excuses for the failure of these pharmacists to warn patients about these interactions. The knowledge base of pharmacists should be sufficient to detect and prevent drug interactions. However, the environment in which pharmacists practice and the systems that support these pharmacists are often deficient.

Who has the responsibility to prevent these interactions—the pharmacist, the physician, or the patient? All members of a patient's healthcare team must work together to provide the optimal care for an individual patient. The pharmacist is the member of the healthcare team who is the medication expert and has the responsibility for detecting medication problems. The patient also has a responsibility for ensuring that the pharmacist has the necessary information to screen for health-related problems effectively. The patient must be willing to ask for and receive counseling from the pharmacist. Patients need to tell the pharmacist about all the medications that they are taking, including over-the-counter medications. One patient may see several physicians—their general practitioners, a cardiac specialist, and an allergist. That is why it is so important for patients to get all of their medications at one pharmacy.

Other Important Concepts

Other points that could be made in answer to this question would include the following factors.

Impact of the Changing Healthcare Environment on the Practice of Pharmacy. As a result of the changing healthcare environment, pharmacists are dispensing more prescriptions which cuts into the time they spend with patients. And prescription drug therapy is being used in lieu of costly hospital care and is more aggressive, powerful, and complex than ever before.

Working Conditions. In some pharmacy practice settings, some issues compromise the ability of the pharmacist to provide care to patients. Examples of these barriers include inadequate staffing, long work hours, an inability to take breaks, and high stress environments. It is the responsibility of employers and managers to design and implement systems that eliminate these barriers and facilitate patient care.

Interaction Warning Systems. When pharmacists process prescription orders electronically, they are often signaled by drug interaction warning programs that are connected to the electronic claims payment system or are part of their internal computer software system. Many of these systems do not effectively differentiate between minor and significant interactions. As a result, these systems "cry wolf" hundreds of times a day for clinically insignificant drug interactions and undermine the credibility of the warning system.

Administrative Tasks. Many administrative tasks that pharmacists are now being asked to complete serve as impediments to caregiving. For just one example, patients are covered by countless prescription drug insurance programs with varied, disorganized, and nonstandard identification cards that are frequently difficult to interpret. Pharmacists are required to interpret this inconsistent information prior to the electronic transmission of a drug claim for payment. As part of the electronic transmission, pharmacists may receive administrative signals and warnings such as formulary noncompliance messages mixed in with clinically significant drug interaction warnings.

Positive Messages

Finally, we created a list of positive points that pharmacists could use in responding to media queries. By doing this, we hoped to help turn a negative event into a positive one. These points included the following:

▶ Make sure that the prescription says what symptoms the prescribed drug is supposed to treat (example, for headache). This information is important because the same drug is often used to treat many different problems. Your pharmacist can monitor treatment much more effectively with this information.

▶ Make sure you understand what your prescription medicines are for and how and when to take them. If patients do not understand, it is important to have a pharmacist review their medications and answer any questions.

▶ Find a pharmacist who will talk with you. If a pharmacist is too busy to talk with you, choose another pharmacist. Pharmacists should be chosen

PERSONAL EXAMPLE

Man Bites Dog

The manufacturer of a controversial dietary supplement turned to the World Wide Web to launch a preemptive strike against a prime-time news story feared to be hostile to its product.

The manufacturer launched a Web site to refute what it believed would be a negative and unfair report on the weight loss product that was scheduled to be aired on *20/20*. The weight-loss product was already under attack because of the side effects associated with one of its ingredients, ephedrine. The company said it would not agree to the interview unless its cameras were allowed in. As a result, both the company and ABC News videotaped the conversation.

Before the TV episode was aired, the company made an unedited version of the 70-minute interview that *20/20* conducted with the company's chief executive and medical director available on its Web site. An edited, 15-minute version of the interview and information about the safety of the product was also made available. The Web site directed visitors to what the company called documentation of its product's safety. A transcript of the interview was also on the site, with various comments and explanation inserted by the company. The site address was plugged into a series of newspaper and radio ads that cost $1.5 million.

This company's attack marked an unusual confrontational effort to strike back. Such a strategy, however, runs the risk of drawing more attention to criticisms about the company. In other words, it flags the issue to millions who might otherwise have missed the debate.

The company believes this was the first time that unedited footage of a TV news magazine interview had been released by a secondary source before broadcast. ABC News questioned whether it might have to impose restrictions on interviews or risk similar preemptive strikes from future subjects who think they won't get a fair shake. This raises the question of whether using the Internet as a tool to fight the news media will become increasingly common.

with care. It is important to build a strong relationship with your pharmacist.

▶ Ask to talk with the pharmacist about your medications when you visit the pharmacy. Ask if the prescription that you are about to take will interact with any medication you are currently taking. This step is important for new prescription orders as well as for renewals and is especially important if you are taking more than one medication. Most interactions are minor, but some are deadly. Consumers must be proactive and demand the care to which they are entitled.

We were able to alert pharmacists that the story was going to air and that it seemed to have this negative angle. By providing this information quickly to the APhA leadership who might be contacted by their local television affiliates for a comment on this story, we were able to contain further negative stories on the local level. Pharmacists were armed and ready to address this issue and since television seems to resurrect this type of story about the profession during "sweeps" periods, the points can be used over and over again.

Summary

The secret to a successful interview is to be in control. By knowing the reporter and the news medium, knowing your subject, and focusing on the main points you want to make, you can increase your chances of controlling the interview, rather than letting it control you.▶

Controlling the Interview: Case Example

You've been asked to do an interview with a reporter who has delusions of grandeur. He believes that his fate is to be the anchor on a TV network news program. He makes no distinction between "hard" and "soft" news. The subject is how pharmacists can help the elderly get the most from their medications. This reporter is looking not for news, but for controversy.

He begins by asking a loaded question: "How can you people take advantage of those poor older folks who have barely enough money to buy food? It's like you're drug pushers with a license. What do you have to say about that?"

Be calm. Buy a little time by saying, "I'm glad you asked that question, Bob." Hold your ground. Then answer, throwing out some statistics prefaced by, "As you know, Bob," or "As you may have read in The New York Times, Bob..." Regardless of how obscure your statistics are, Bob will probably pretend he knows about them. But do not lie. There's always a listener who will catch you at it.

Should You Use a Public Relations Firm?

The first five chapters of this book discussed the tools you need to develop and implement a public relations program for your pharmacy practice. If you don't have the time or the inclination, and you do have some money to spend, you may want to consider hiring a firm to do your public relations for you.

The purpose of this chapter is to discuss how to select a public relations firm or freelancer to support your public relations goals. It includes tips on what to look for in a public relations firm and questions to ask when you are interviewing candidates. If you've already engaged the services of a public relations firm, this information can help you judge if it is doing the best job for you. The chapter concludes with some advice on hiring freelancers, who may be appropriate for more modest public relations initiatives.

Do It Yourself or Not? It's Up to You

You must decide whether you or someone on your staff has the capability, time, and interest to perform all of the functions of publicity. It's a big responsibility. It entails maintaining good relations on an ongoing basis with the media and sending them a regular supply of news releases. News-making activities must be generated and feature stories must be developed.

The Case for Outside Help

Do-it-yourself public relations may be difficult for pharmacists for many reasons. Time is perhaps the most important consideration. Most pharmacists want to spend their time providing pharmaceutical care—that's where their training and interests lie. From this perspective, a large practice might be in better shape than a smaller one. A larger practice site may well have a talented and capable person on the staff to whom the publicity responsibility can be assigned without significantly interfering with other work.

Another reason that pharmacists may be reluctant to do their own public relations is a natural reluctance to being put in the position of "blowing one's own horn." An agency, they reason, can sometimes do the job more effectively and professionally. The staffs of public relations agencies maintain ongoing relations with members of the media. They're in the business of selling story ideas and channeling news. They're not exactly a disinterested third party, because they are on your payroll; at the same time, they're in the business of "tooting horns" and feel comfortable doing it.

The Case for "Do-It-Yourself" Public Relations

Because the technical skills needed in publicity are not as elaborate as those used in advertising, it is possible to accomplish a great deal internally. A pharmacist with a small practice requires nothing but the intelligence and time to follow the basic procedures outlined in this book. A bright, personable, and imaginative pharmacist can handle some programs and publicity activities as effectively as an agency can.

Doing your own public relations usually also saves money. Modest efforts carried out by staff are less expensive than those that entail the services of a freelance writer or a public relations firm.

Think of it this way: the same entrepreneurial outlook that makes you a good pharmacist can enable you to master the basics of public relations, learn how to develop basic tools such as news releases, and establish good relations with key reporters and editors, in other words, to mount a small-scale publicity program.

Advantages of Doing Your Own PR

There are several advantages to running a publicity program internally.

An inside person is constantly in touch with your operation. He or she knows your practice, knows the profession, and has the opportunity to see newsworthy activities as they develop.

An internal program gives you greater control over both the focus of public relations and its activities. You know what's going on at all times, how much time is being spent on the program, and what the media reaction is at any given moment.

Doing your own public relations probably will be less expensive than hiring a firm. However, this is not always the case; for example, the time a staff person allocates to publicity might well add up to more dollars than the cost of an outside agency. Doing it internally does not mean doing it for free.

Don't forget that there's also a middle ground. An internal program does not have to be totally self-sustaining. It can be supplemented with specialists as needed. For example, a photographer or writer can be hired on a project-by-project basis.

Advantages of Hiring a Public Relations Firm

The staff members of public relations firms are specialists. Public relations is their business, and the full focus of their business is serving their clients in public relations activities.

An agency is staffed and organized to deal with all aspects of a public relations program. It's equipped for the quick dissemination of releases, as well as for direct contact with the media. It maintains up-to-the-minute mailing lists and lists of appropriate personnel in the media.

PR firms have well-established relationships with the media.

A good agency brings to each program the extent of its experience. This experience is the result of having served many organizations with a wide variety of needs and therefore having developed broad experience in effective problem solving.

Agencies are objective. A good agency provides both objectivity and advocacy. One is of no use without the other. The agency will use its objectivity to help you make realistic public relations decisions.

Finally, the cost of using an agency, if the contract is negotiated properly, is predictable. While there may be hidden overhead factors to be added to the cost of an internal public relations person, the expense of an external agency can be budgeted.

Working with a Firm

If you decide to hire a public relations agency, you must realize that this doesn't let you off the hook. You must communicate your public relations goals to the agency staff and work with them to make the program succeed. You must develop a close working relationship with the person assigned to your account and be responsive to his or her needs. The media will quickly discern the degree of authority your public relations person has in speaking for your organization and in serving as a source of real news. You must have a genuine commitment both to the program and to the person you hire to do it.

Before you retain a public relations firm, you must know what you want to achieve. The first step in the search for a public relations firm is to identify and prioritize your organizational goals. Later, these goals can be shared with the firm you choose. These goals will become the basis for determining your public relations goals and objectives. Your public relations firm will use these to develop strategies, tactics, and tasks oriented to your specific needs.

You must also decide whether you want that firm to handle your entire public relations program or just its publicity. A firm that handles publicity sees to it that an organization's products or services receive media coverage in the form of articles or radio and television broadcasts. When a firm handles public relations as a whole, its job is to help craft an organization's image. Most public relations firms do both.

What a Public Relations Firm Can Do for You

▶ Provide an outside viewpoint or perspective.

▶ Increase an organization's overall visibility.

▶ Support an entire marketing effort.

▶ Counsel in a crisis.

▶ Strengthen community relations.

▶ Critique existing organization policies as they affect public relations goals.

▶ Measure and evaluate existing public relations programs.

▶ Bring new skills to complement existing public relations efforts.

Identifying Potential Candidates

Once your specific communication needs have been determined, choosing the right public relations firm involves a certain amount of investigation. Public relations agencies come in all sizes and forms. They range from the one-person firm to major national firms with offices in many cities throughout the country. Many advertising agencies have departments that may be one person or full-scale public relations staffs.

The appropriate agency is the one that meets your needs and can work within your budget. If your program—and your budget—are small, then conceivably a one-person agency can perform as successfully for you as can a large, major national firm. If your program is more substantial, it will require the resources of a larger firm.

To start with, talk with your peers—friends, business acquaintances, and fellow members of business or civic groups. Find out if their organizations retain public relations firms. If so, which ones? Are their performances satisfactory? Would they recommend them? What do you know about any other public relations firms in the area?

If you are a member of a professional association, ask its leaders to recommend public relations firms in the area that they know by reputation or experience.

Call local newspaper, television, and radio reporters who cover health, and ask about the public relations firms from whom they receive the most accurate and professional information and materials. Make the same query of editors of trade publications that cover pharmacy. Most media can name several public relations firms and also can rank them for you. Remember, however, that the media's opinions about public relations firms' capabilities are generally based on or confined to just one area of public relations—publicity.

After polling some peers, professional associations, and media, you probably will have heard some firm names several times, an indication that they are perhaps firms you should investigate further.

The Screening Process

Make a list of the firms that your initial screening indicates are good candidates. Next, contact a principal at each firm by telephone or letter. Describe your organization and its public relations needs. Ask if the firm would be interested in talking with you. If it is, check to make sure it does not already represent a client that might be a conflict of interest.

If the firm's response sounds promising, ask the principal to send a letter with the firm's general background and any experience in the pharmacy area, its range of services, the depth of professional qualifications the firm's principals and staff has, specialized skills or resources, its current client list, and the firm's policies on charging for its services.

Taking a Closer Look

After reviewing the responses from the public relations firms contacted, select those that seem to best fit your public relations needs and set up a meeting at the offices of each firm.

Interview several firms; don't allow yourself to be sold by just one. The relationship with a public relations firm is a close one—closer perhaps than with an advertising agency. A great deal depends upon a strong interplay of communication and ideas.

During the interview, be on the lookout for the following qualities.

Questions to Ask Before Beginning to Search for a Public Relations Firm

▶ How extensive a public relations effort do you want to undertake? Which of the media do you need your agency to handle?

▶ How much money do you have to spend?

▶ Do you want a company with a particular philosophy or one that is willing to work with the philosophy of its clients?

▶ Who will be your pharmacy's liaison with the firm?

▶ What reporting or measurement methods will you use?

Creativity

Look for creative ideas that hit the target. If you find them, you will know that the people you are considering can think on their feet.

Experience with Similar Programs

What counts in the long run is the ability of your public relations people to design and implement a program that addresses your particular need. If it's a

The Preliminary Interview: What to Look for

The Public Relations Society of America recommends that organizations hiring a public relations firm explore the following questions during the preliminary interview:

What are the size and nature of the firm? How many clients does it have and who are they? Are many of the clients the same size as your organization? What businesses are its clients in?

What successful programs for other clients can it show you? The firm's response should include a full presentation of the original objectives, the program designed to meet those objectives, and clear evidence of the successful performance of those programs.

How well established is the firm? A public relations agency is a business, just as yours is. It should be able to demonstrate that it's well established and financially sound. Getting a Dun & Bradstreet rating is helpful.

What is the experience and what are the qualifications of the people who will work on your account? Are they senior people? Can you see samples of their work? What's the line of internal reporting responsibility? Who in the agency has the ultimate responsibility for performance on your account?

Who will be working directly on your account, and what are his or her experience and qualifications? Do you personally like the account executive to be assigned to you? Since the working relationship will be close, this is extremely important.

What is the fee structure, including the policy on out-of-pocket expenses?

What contractual arrangements are offered? Agencies prefer a year's contract. This is understandable and usually acceptable, provided that there is a three-month trial period and a 30-day cancellation clause.

Do they ask the right questions? Even in a preliminary conversation you can tell pretty quickly whether you're dealing with intelligent people who understand your profession and who can quickly learn your public relations problems, your objectives, and the role that they will be expected to play in your program.

What references do they offer? These references should include both present clients and business references. If possible, the firm should include references from the media. A well-established public relations firm should be happy to give you the names of several editors with whom it has long-standing relationships and who can vouch for its professionalism.

marketing need, look for people who have done it for other groups similar to yours. If you need grass-roots public relations to turn around the state legislature, make sure that the people you hire have a solid track record in that field. A background in your particular profession would be desirable, but not essential.

Strong Management

No matter whom you hire, the people who begin your program may not be around six months or a year later. Turnover is high in public relations. Be sure that a strong management team exists to keep the program on track in the event of turnover.

Credentials

You would be surprised to learn how seldom people check out claims made by public relations firms or professionals they hire. Find out if the programs presented as agency experience were as successful as they were made to sound. Determine if individuals who worked on them will be involved in your program.

During the initial visit, also look for:

▶ How the firm presents its general capabilities and focuses on your specific needs.

▶ Whether you are offered an opportunity to talk with senior members of the firm. These individuals must be clear about your goals in order to provide appropriate support. Once your relationship with a firm begins, they will assign an account representative, who will be your routine contact with the firm.

▶ The firm's familiarity with the buzzwords of pharmacy and references to trends in your field—a good indication of previous experience or homework done.

Be sure to ask how long it will take the account representative who will be assigned to work with you to get up to speed on your account. Also ask about the internal reporting methods used. Finally, ask who the key backup person will be when your account representative is not available?

During your visit you might be asked what other firms you are talking with. It is perfectly appropriate to provide this information, and you should not feel uncomfortable about doing so.

Visiting the offices of the top contenders, hearing their presentations, and talking with senior members should enable you to narrow your search to two or three firms. Now is the time to request that each set up a meeting for you with those who would be the principal players on your organization's account team. In doing so, also ask each public relations firm to send a written proposal outlining how it would provide the public relations services your organization needs.

Agency Fees

Once you have discussed your public relations goals and strategies, it should be possible for any company or experienced public relations firm to develop a fairly accurate budget for the program. You will need to discuss fees and charges in general during the interviewing process. You may find that rates differ substantially. Cost should be one factor, but not the sole factor, that you use in selecting the agency that will represent you.

Once you've selected the firm that you believe will do the best job for you, you will negotiate a contract. This is an important activity. It begins with your own awareness of what your public relations goals are, what you need, and, in some cases, what you can do yourself. Don't pay a firm for built-in extras you don't need. Carefully analyze the quality of professionals you are offered and the amount of time they will spend on your account. Many firms promise senior staff to work on your account but deliver junior people who may be learning the business on your time.

Don't expect to hire good talent at bargain rates. Make sure your budget is reasonable. Guard against gouging by securing competitive proposals and costs on similar programs.

There are several options in billing for services, and based on its initial perception of your needs, your public relations firm will recommend one of them. Firms are generally paid in one of four ways: a flat fee, a retainer fee, a minimum monthly fee, or a project fee.

Flat Fee

A firm may charge a flat fee—that is, an hourly fee, for all services rendered. Each month's bill itemizes the amount of time spent by each agency executive in each of the categories in which he or she is functioning for the organization.

Retainer Fee

Under this arrangement, in return for payment of a mutually agreed-upon monthly fee, members of the public relations firm will be available to assist you whenever needed. You pay a flat rate fee that is billed in advance each month, whether or not any services are used. The retainer fee is reviewed periodically to determine whether any adjustments are needed based on use of services.

This arrangement works well for organizations that have their own communication capabilities but need counseling for complex communication questions or periodic help with specialized tasks such as speech writing.

These arrangements can also result in a more productive relationship. Your agency can devote more creative time and research time without worrying about the meter eating up your budget. However, you should be sure that you are getting all that you pay for, including the time of top professionals who were promised at the outset.

Minimum Monthly Fee

A public relations firm may establish a minimum monthly fee for its services based on the number of hours per month it estimates will be spent on your account. This minimum is billed in advance to the client each month, and members of the public relations firm charge their time against that minimum based on their individual hourly rates.

If the hours worked exceed the monthly minimum fee, the client's next bill will include the cost of the previous month's additional time. If an organization wishes to be notified that the hours worked in any given month will exceed the monthly minimum so it can have the option of deferring an activity or task to another month, it can so specify; this requirement should be included in the letter of agreement.

The minimum monthly fee arrangement is ideal for organizations that may need a variety of specialized services with time requirements that differ from month to month.

Project Fee

Public relations services for a one-time project, such as the opening ceremony for a new building, may be provided for a set fee that may include both services and expenses.

Some firms may decline to undertake a project under such a fee arrangement if their estimate of the hours and out-of-pocket costs involved indicates that the project budget ceiling is too low. Others may be willing to take on the assignment to open the door to further work with the prospect or if they believe the organization is one whose addition to their client roster would make any time expended beyond the budget ceiling a worthwhile investment.

Miscellaneous Expenses

Prior to signing a contract with a public relations firm, you should have a general idea of the cost of a variety of miscellaneous expenses. For example, how much are reproduction costs for releases and other material? How large a mailing list is involved, and what will the mailing costs generally be? If the public relations firm is located any distance from your practice, who pays the travel expenses for meetings with you?

Other expenses to negotiate include:

- Out-of-pocket and routine expenses
- Clipping services
- Photography and art
- Telephone
- Special wire services for rapid distribution of urgent news

▶ Transportation other than for meetings with you
▶ Promotional expenses for meeting with the media, including media entertainment
▶ Postage, courier, and overnight delivery charges
▶ Messenger services
▶ Photocopying
▶ Subscriptions to trade publications
▶ Administrative staff overtime on special projects

Contingency Funds

Even in the best-planned program, situations frequently arise, often in the form of opportunities, for special projects or activities. Such situations may include an opportunity for someone in your practice to participate as a panelist in a seminar or the need for a special brochure or pamphlet. While these occasions are normally unexpected and unbudgeted, their extra costs can often be measured in terms of added value. Your budget should be sufficiently flexible to permit these unexpected expenses.

Important Details

Regardless of the fee arrangement selected, it is important to know how a public relations firm accounts for its time. The firm should outline for you the type of written monthly activity reports it provides to its clients. Information provided by a public relations firm during fee discussions should also include such billing policy details as:

▶ Minimum time segment charges (hour, half hour, quarter hour)
▶ Maximum amount of chargeable time per day
▶ Method of billing travel time
▶ Commission or markup percentages, if any
▶ Interest charge percentage, if any, on balances over 30 days past due

A Final Word

Guard against paying for extras offered by a public relations firm that you don't need or for overly elaborate products like videotapes, films, or expensive brochures that don't fit the strategy.

At the same time, you do need to be flexible. Conditions change and your program must respond to meet unforeseen challenges and opportunities. You may choose to place a planned activity on the back burner and replace it with a new one requiring approximately the same costs. If the bottom line is significantly more work either for in-house staff or an outside firm, something has to give.

Working Effectively with Your Public Relations Firm

Dealing with your public relations firm can be very different from dealing with your ad agency. In advertising, once the program is set, it's executed in a series of ads and promotional activities. Each ad can be seen and judged and, to some degree, its effectiveness can be measured.

A Day-by-Day Enterprise

A public relations program, on the other hand, is an ongoing activity with a constant flow of ideas and a day-by-day effort to establish workable media relations, newsworthy activities, releases, feature articles, and other events or items.

The relationship with your public relations firm begins with a clear-cut program spelled out on paper so that you know at the outset exactly what your agency is going to do for you, and the timetable within which it's going to do it. Your public relations account executive should have constant access to you and your staff, without, of course, interfering with your day-to-day activities. If you're not experienced in public relations, his or her job is to train you to understand what kinds of material and activities the agency needs to know to do its job. You should expect new and fresh ideas regularly from your agency.

You should also expect periodic meetings (at least once a week) with your account executive to review the week's activities and the status of the program. If the firm is large enough, the account executive's supervisor should also meet with you periodically to review your program.

Written reports, no matter how brief, should be forthcoming regularly, and notes should be taken at each meeting. Having such a record avoids misunderstandings about what was promised and what was delivered.

The difficult part of a public relations program is that it takes time and a great deal of work before the results begin to show up. Unfortunately, this is more often true with a smaller organization than with a larger one, because a smaller company is less likely to generate the kinds of activities that are newsworthy.

Need for Persistence

Be patient. No program you undertake should last less than three months. This period should be time enough for a new agency to become familiar with your practice, to prepare any necessary materials, and to develop some successful publicity. The nature of publicity is such that you can't always pick your dates and timing. A great many releases may have to go to an editor, over a long period, before he or she decides that you've said something newsworthy, or even before the editor decides to accept your organization as a news source. Feature material may also take a month to six weeks to develop and place.

In publicity, you hear the word "no" more often than you do "yes," and it sometimes takes a great stream of material to the media before a single clipping is produced. In the start-up period of a publicity program, the results may be slim but the effort isn't wasted. Contacts are being made on your behalf and a familiarity with your organization is being developed—all of which should pay off in the next three months.

Looking for Results

Even though results may not be apparent as quickly as you would wish, they should eventually appear. The program and the agency's activities must be carefully monitored even during that initial period to be sure that the pipeline is in fact being filled and that the time isn't being used by the agency just to learn your operation and your profession on your money.

If, during the three-month initial period, you don't quickly discern that your agency is coming to understand your organization and is functioning successfully on your behalf, or if at the end of six months there have been no tangible results as measured against the original public relations program, then it's time to consider whether you've chosen the right agency. Any questions you have of this nature should be raised directly with the agency principals. If the program isn't working, this failure should be discussed with the agency frankly. They may not have made clear to you what they're trying to accomplish and how they work, or you may not be cooperating with them in areas that count. There may be personality problems with the particular account executive, or the agency itself may not be the right one for you. If a program isn't working, it's the program and its performance that's at fault—not the validity of public relations and publicity as a marketing tool.

What's Your Standard of Success?

Once a program is under way, it's easy to be overly impressed by a good article or an appearance on a network talk show. These are signs your program is on track. But they must be viewed as the means to the end.

Before you begin your program, decide what it must achieve to be successful and express that standard in measurable terms. A certain percentage increase in business? Defeat of legislation? Measurable attitudinal changes? Before you start, let your public relations counsel tell you whether your expectations are reasonable, given the resources you are willing to spend. Then decide together upon adjusting your objectives, if you need to.

Measure results against your objectives. Activity, in and of itself, is not enough. Are these activities accomplishing the attitudinal changes they are meant to? If not, your strategy may be flawed or the environment of opinion may have changed since you began the program. Is there objective evidence that attitudes are improving among key audiences?

Using Freelancers

If the scope of your publicity program is limited, it may be economical to use freelancers or a writing service rather than to retain a public relations firm. If your needs in some areas are only tactical—for example, an occasional release or exclusive feature story—a freelance writer is ideal.

Don't be worried if the candidate is not a pharmacist. Good journalists have been trained to be quick studies. They can write on a number of subjects with little help. If you can provide the proper background, the right sources, and the right directions, a good writer will produce good copy. I have used freelancers quite successfully. Most of these writers have become experts in the areas they are covering after doing only a couple of stories.

You might even want to consider whether your entire program could be managed by freelancers. Unless the individual whom you hire is extremely experienced in pharmacy, more responsibility for developing story ideas, placing the story in the right media, and providing good direction would rest with you and your staff under this arrangement than if you were working with a public relations firm. You might also want to use an agency for special events and promotions.

How to Locate Candidates

If you have a communications program, chances are that some freelancers have already contacted you. Review their résumés and clips. If you don't have any résumés on file, call your local newspaper. They may use freelancers periodically. They may also be aware of the names of retired journalists in the area or writers who contribute to other area publications.

▶ Check with the Chamber of Commerce, hospitals, nonprofit organizations, and state or local business publications. Many publish newsletters or have someone doing publicity, often on a part-time basis. Call the mayor's press secretary for a suggestion. Think of organizations that might need publicity assistance, and ask for recommendations.

▶ Check the candidate's writing ability first by reviewing samples of published work.

▶ Call in the most promising candidates for interviews.

▶ Check writers' fees. They should be low compared with those of an agency, because their overhead is much less. They may charge by the hour, the day, or the page. If the writer is to travel for you, be sure he or she follows your own company's travel policy.

Summary

Good public relations is good public relations—whether it's done by a pharmacist or a veteran public relations professional. Engage the services of a firm or a freelancer if you wish; however, be aware that you'll still have to be involved in the process. That means hiring the best firm, communicating and formulating your public relations strategy, and being available to answer their questions and follow through on opportunities they have identified for you.▶

CHAPTER 7

Getting Involved in Your Community

Many pharmacists who have sharpened their merchandising skills in an increasingly competitive marketplace still do not realize that community public relations efforts are just as important as marketing plans.

If you want to have good relations in your community, you have to know more about your community, and the community has to know more about you. Community relations begin as an attitude—a desire to serve the community in any way that's appropriate for you and the community. It may mean lecturing on how to make medications work better, sponsoring a local community health campaign, or featuring a drug a week on your Web site. The important thing to remember is that you are in business in your community, and no matter what the scope of your practice, the more favorably your community views you as a good citizen, the more business you're going to do. It's difficult to place a price tag on the value of good community relations—until you find out you don't have any.

This chapter describes what pharmacists can do to become more visible in their communities. It covers such tried-and-true community relations techniques as special events, speeches, health fairs, and newsletters.

Your Community Needs You

Today's patients control much of their own healthcare. Increased awareness of healthcare issues prompts them to ask questions and demand more information. Patients also have a broad choice in the selection of types of pharmacies and pharmaceutical care services. They are likely to go from pharmacy to pharmacy in search of one that provides them with what they perceive as good healthcare.

Why should a patient select your pharmacy over any other? What do you offer that is different or more desirable than that of any other pharmacist? Most pharmacists will accept the desirability of knowledge and skill, coupled with one-on-one counseling with patients, but time constraints limit the amount that actually takes place. Whenever a pharmacist appears before a group, the counseling potential is multiplied.

To everyone whom you serve in your capacity as a pharmacist, you *are* the profession of pharmacy. How you talk, what you say, your appearance, your every action projects your image as a pharmacist.

You can find many opportunities to put yourself in the forefront of the public eye. It takes only a little effort. If you practice pharmaceutical care, you need to practice public relations.

To meet patients' needs for information and to enhance your professional status within the community, there is no better public relations device than lectures or presentations made before groups in the community. Pharmacists making such presentations are soon perceived as experts in the field of medications. Their willingness to perform a public service is also appreciated.

Don't forget that, although building your own goodwill with the public is the major goal of community public relations, it also offers an opportunity to collaborate with other pharmacists and health professionals. Collaboration increases the impact of an event and makes it more successful. You may want to have some events on your own and participate in others that are jointly planned.

Community Relations—Many Opportunities

Your prime purpose for practicing pharmacy is to serve your community's health needs. Serving your patients properly is essential for guaranteeing their continued loyalty. In addition to your pharmaceutical expertise and professionalism, a good relationship with patients is based on courtesy, friendliness, dependability, understanding, honesty, and a sincere desire to serve.

Community activities and involvement demonstrate civic spirit and increase your visibility. By being active in your local service clubs, professional associations, disease support groups, activities for older citizens, or religious organizations, you show your concern to community members.

Begin with your own staff and employees. This step involves more than just a matter of maintaining good morale. Remember that, at the end of a business day, your employees go home and talk about your practice to their family and friends. If they're happy to work there, if they like the way you do business, they will enhance your reputation. And certainly in any public relations attitude you develop, your staff will take the lead from you.

Next, reach out to areas that you are already closest to. Membership in civic and service clubs, for example, offers an excellent means for meeting the leaders of the community. Active participation in such professional projects as National Pharmacy Week, Poison Prevention Week, and diabetes detection campaigns are a must for the pharmacist who wants to promote a professional image (see Chapter 8).

Fulfilling public speaking engagements before schools and religious and civic groups increases your visibility and establishes you as an expert in the healthcare arena.

You should also make yourself available on a routine basis as a media source—a person the media seek as a guest for talk shows, an expert for news interviews, and a resource for background information on news or feature stories.

Good community relations has a "snowball effect." After giving one or two successful presentations, you will find yourself trying to accommodate requests from others who have heard you directly or have heard of you. Your public relations program has become self-perpetuating!

Potential Audiences

As already indicated, the possibilities for community programs are virtually endless. Here are some examples of audiences that you may want to target.

Civic Groups

Contact officers in local clubs and volunteer to make presentations to their members or to the public under their sponsorship. Such organizations include the Rotary Club, Elks Club, Lions Club, and women's groups.

Neighborhood Groups

Make every social contact a potential audience. If you are talking to your neighbor about his teenage children, volunteer to have a neighborhood "fireside chat" where you will present information concerning a topic of concern such as drug abuse.

Schools

Contact teachers in public and private schools and volunteer your time to talk to a class on topics of interest, such as drug abuse education. Other contacts include principals, room parents, and PTA officers.

Places of Worship

Volunteer your services in the local places of worship. Visit the religious leaders in your area and present your topics and ideas.

Disease-Specific Groups

Patients with chronic diseases generally experience long-term discomfort and disability. Many times they experience a rapid decline in self-esteem and depression. As the pathology progresses, they often take numerous medications and frequently experience bad effects. To combat these physiological and psychosocial stresses, they seek peer support. Groups may be formed locally and supported by hospitals or they may operate as local chapters of a national organization. They meet frequently and want accurate and relevant information concerning their disease and therapeutic regimen.

"Golden" Opportunities

Older Americans are becoming one of the largest groups of consumers. Their needs are complex and call for innovative ideas. Businesses and associations can benefit by tailoring services that emphasize wellness and prevention. Pharmacy programs should recognize, however, that the mature consumer can be a discriminating customer—one who is open only to a product or service that adds genuine value to his or her life.

Survey the older residents in your area and find out what is important to them. Potential ways for reaching the mature consumer include, for example, providing services and detailed product information, marketing videos and large-print publications, and using toll-free telephone lines and hot lines for answering questions. Keep in mind that Internet use is growing among older people; make sure your Web site is relevant to them. You may also sponsor seminars that target older citizens. Note: In doing so, be careful when using titles such as "seniors," which some may find offensive.

Here are two examples of copy a pharmacy might use to promote seminars to older Americans.

Managing Your Medications

Do you know how to take your medications effectively and safely? Do you know what to do to prevent problems when using medications? Join us for an informative and worthwhile session on medications. Learn how drugs can aid the body's natural defenses to promote recovery. Practical tips and guidelines for taking medications will be discussed, as well as suggestions for getting the most beneficial results from your medications. If you can't join us in person, look for this information on our Web site.

Diabetes Fair

Learn about meal planning, exercise, blood sugar monitoring, diabetes medicines, and more—all the areas you are concerned about for keeping your blood sugar in good control and preventing long-term complications of diabetes. Bring your blood glucose monitor for cleaning. Gloucester Healthcare Center, Anderson's Pharmacy, and pharmaceutical companies will provide displays.

Enhancing Your Public Identity

Here are details on some strategies that can enhance your position in your community.

How to Be Viewed as an Expert

At the heart of a good community public relations campaign is your expertise—expertise that you agree to share in a variety of contexts. Here are some ways that you can build public credibility in your expertise.

Earn the media's trust. If a reporter is on deadline and calls you for a quick quote, be direct and to the point. If you're sensitive to the needs of reporters, they'll be sure to call back.

Send out substantive news releases. Trendy and timely news releases are a good means of improving your visibility as an authority on medications.

Hit the keyboard. If you're comfortable with the written word, you might also consider writing a column or an article for a local publication. A word of caution: this can require a great deal of work. Unless you're a proficient writer, tread cautiously here.

Give some speeches. Public speaking and community involvement can help you become better known.

At the onset, being perceived as an expert takes some self-promotion. Follow these tips, but remain alert to additional opportunities for exposure. Once your reputation begins to grow, you may well find that the media won't leave you alone.

Ongoing Programs and Projects

Establish information or assistance programs that profile your practice and activities. For example, you could hold monthly sessions with patients about the medications they are taking and how these drugs might interact with over-the-counter products as well as with vitamins and herbal remedies.

Special Activities

Examples of special activities and events include anniversary celebrations, introduction of new products or services, providing a platform for a prominent speaker, and seminars and annual meetings.

Speeches

Develop a few "stump speeches" on topics of broad interest, such as drug interactions. Be prepared, too, to develop speeches on special topics of timely interest. Tailor your speech to audience needs—for example, gender, age, and educational background.

Special Events

A special event serves several purposes. It promotes goodwill within the community, builds visibility for your practice, and provides the opportunity for possible publicity. However, staging a special event can be costly, and the results are never guaranteed. When you're trying to

PERSONAL EXAMPLE

Good Plans Go Awry— Despite the Balloons

When I was handling the public relations for a caterer in Washington, D.C., we decided to hold the business's 50th anniversary party on the National Mall in Washington. We had an enormous tent erected (after "going through fire" to get permits from the city), invited the diplomatic corps and the Washington media, and provided exotic food and entertainment. We even had tents set up as elegantly appointed "powder rooms" for the guests. (Portable facilities never looked so good.)

We left no detail unattended. For example, we coordinated with the air traffic control center at Washington National Airport because we were going to release Mylar balloons during the event and we did not want them to interfere with the airplanes landing and taking off at the airport. In each of the balloons was a message to whoever found it to contact the caterer, who would send them a gift. (By the way, the furthest location that we heard from was Nova Scotia. Several children found a balloon in a field and sent a letter to the caterer.)

Judging by the size of the crowds, our event was an unequivocal success. However, we got very little postevent media coverage. Why not?

Unfortunately, at the same time our party was occurring, the President was appearing at the White House at a spontaneous ceremony. The event was not on the schedule when we began planning our event. When editors were faced with deciding whether to cover an anniversary party or a Presidential ceremony, the head of state won.

There is no way to prevent something like that from happening. (If it hadn't been the President, it might have been a bomb threat that commanded the attention of the print reporters and TV crews.) All in all, we viewed the anniversary party as a success. We had attracted the attention of potential clients—those in the diplomatic community who would use the services of this caterer. Although we would have liked postevent publicity, we had accomplished our primary goal. We did send out news releases after the event as we received feedback from people who had found the anniversary balloons. That proved to be a unique human interest story.

get coverage of an event being held on a special day at a special time, it makes it all the more difficult to predict how much news coverage you might receive. In fact, many special events get no postevent coverage, as illustrated in the example on the previous page.

One final note about special events or any other activity: Although you may need commercial sponsorship, be wary of it. An event that has commercial overtones may be perceived as advertising by the media or by the public. Not only may it not generate media coverage, it may also be counterproductive and create negative, rather than positive, public opinion.

Guidelines for Executing a Special Event

Special events can have successful outcomes, regardless of whether they receive media coverage. If you do get media coverage, all the better. Here are some ideas for planning and promoting such a special pharmacy-oriented community event.

Early Planning. Determine the purpose, audience, and theme of the event. You may, for example, want to tie in your event to another event, such as a holiday or historical happening, an athletic competition, or a charitable fundraiser. In developing a plan, include the role of volunteers and staff. Be specific on responsibilities and accountability.

If there are local celebrities who can become involved in the event, they may be able to draw the attention of the media. The mayor or council members are obvious choices; others include local radio or television personalities who have an interest in your cause. Be careful, however, about doing a "stunt." There is always the chance that it will backfire.

Pick an accessible, visible location.

Check the local calendars to make sure your event will not conflict with any others that are already planned. If any city or local permits are necessary, make arrangements to secure them.

Start advance publicity early so your event will be on the media's radar screen. Think carefully about timing: if you hold your event on a weekend, the media will be working with a skeleton crew.

Allocate adequate financial and human resources to the project, agree on a budget, and get the budget approved. Set a realistic time schedule.

Advanced Planning. As the date nears, look at your checklists and assign specific responsibilities. Be sure to cover the following areas:

▶ Media relations

▶ Printed materials

▶ Speaker confirmations

▶ Liaison with vendors and caterers

▶ Preparation of participants' materials (for example, name tags, seating arrangements, agendas, biographies, honorariums, and thank you correspondence)

Schedule several meetings as the event nears. Two weeks prior to the event, create a detailed schedule; then check it periodically to determine if responsibilities are being met.

Last Minute Activities. One week prior to the event, you will probably need to work intensively with volunteers and staff to make sure that all planned activities are proceeding as scheduled and that no unanticipated problems have arisen.

The day before the event and the day of the event, staff members and key volunteers will live and breathe the event. Such enthusiasm and commitment are vital to the successful execution of special events.

Specific Types of Special Events

Charity Events. Such events could include anything from a holiday party at the local children's hospital to an event marking an annual fundraising drive. Because these are noncommercial events, the media feel comfortable about covering them; however, with or without such coverage, you'll be generating goodwill.

Participation in these events may, in fact, be an excellent "backdoor" approach to getting publicity. Many nonprofit or community organizations have newsletters or belong to national associations which have magazines or newsletters. If you perform a public service for one of these organizations, you may receive coverage in its bulletin or newsletter.

Ceremonies and Open Houses. Ceremonies and open houses are other types of special events. Generally, attendance is by invitation only. If you're having an open house, send invitations to business associates and consumers. If you get publicity and members of the public come, that's fine, but your open house will be a success with or without publicity.

The same holds true for ceremonies. If an occasion is worth marking with a special ceremony, some important people probably will attend. If the public should come, all the better, but you will not be depending on them for the turnout.

Workshops, Screenings, and Clinics. Events such as these are excellent means of building goodwill.

You may want to plan a "brown bag" medicine review at your pharmacy. Invite people to bring in all their medicines. Have pharmacists available for a personal consultation to ensure that the individual is not storing expired medications or is not taking a combination of medications that could cause adverse effects. Depending on what is going on in the news that day, these events might make an excellent backdrop for a local TV news story.

If your pharmacy has a disease state management specialty, such as lipid screening or asthma or diabetes management, have a one-day free screening or clinic and invite the public. Again, the photo opportunities—of you and your staff interacting with the public—may be just what the local health reporter is looking for.

Health Promotion Programs. Your pharmacy may sponsor a variety of community health promotion programs. For example:

▶ Asthma Education Classes—Hold an educational program regularly that teaches participants how to recognize the "triggers" and symptoms of asthma and how to take control of the disease.

▶ Cholesterol, Fats, and the Heart-Healthy Lifestyle—Hold a cardiac education program that focuses on learning about cholesterol, fats, understanding food labels, and exercise. Teach participants how to make low-fat food choices that can reduce their risk of heart disease, stroke, cancer, and diabetes.

▶ Diabetes Health Fair—Plan to hold this event during November, which is American Diabetes Month. Staffed with pharmacists, registered nurses, and dietitians, the health fair could feature booths with information about medication management, hypo/hyperglycemia, stress management, nutrition, exercise, and home glucose monitoring. You may also want to include facilities for testing blood pressure and conducting foot and vision screenings.

▶ Flu Clinics—Flu clinics, most appropriately held in October, are an excellent way of educating the public about the risks of influenza and offering low-cost immunizations.

▶ Smoking Cessation—You can hold a smoking-cessation program using materials from the American Cancer Society.

Getting Media Coverage for Your Community Public Relations Efforts

If you are doing good community public relations, chances are that the media will know and come to you. As a public relations savvy practitioner, however, you probably realize that it's a good idea not to rely on chance but to build efforts to attract media coverage into your activities from the beginning. Media coverage is not essential to good community public relations, but it is a great advantage.

Your promotional campaign can include all the ideas suggested in Chapter 4 and then some—namely, news releases, wire service coverage, media kits, photography, brochures, invitations, and letters. A memorable theme including art work or a logo can help create an awareness of the event and enhance visibility for you long after the particular event is held.

Here are some guidelines on how to secure media coverage for community events.

Planning

Before you promote your pharmacy's specific activities, answer the following questions:

▶ What is your goal, and how can the media help you reach it?

▶ Whom do you want to reach with your program?

▶ Which media can best help you reach your target audience? Are those media credible with the chosen audience?

▶ Is your angle interesting or challenging enough for the media to report?

Timing

If media coverage is important to you, the time at which you schedule the event is equally important. Make sure that the event is at a time convenient for news people.

For example, TV reporters are generally trying to make a 5 or 6 p.m. deadline for the early evening news, while print journalists would have a bit more leeway for the next day's paper. In addition, a print reporter may write the story from a general, human interest standpoint so that the story could run several days after the event. Television reporters, by contrast, tend to want to report an event as it happens.

Therefore, if you would like your event to be covered by the early evening television news, you should schedule it for early in the day—any time until about 3 p.m. If the nature of your event dictates that it be held in the evening, you may try to get coverage on the late news.

Weekend or holiday events have pros and cons. On the plus side, these tend to be quiet news days, and the media are often looking for interesting stories. However, your competition can be tough. For example, on a holiday your community may have one or two events that are held annually. These regular events, rather than a new promotional event with which the media are unfamiliar, tend to be the ones that are covered. Another factor for concern when scheduling an event for a weekend—particularly Sunday—or a holiday is that stations are often operating with a "skeleton" staff. There may not be personnel available to cover your story.

News Releases and Other Publicity Materials

Once you have answered these questions to your satisfaction, you have several media options to help promote your practice. You can issue news releases, media advisories, or feature articles (see Chapter 4).

Send a news release to newspapers or magazines that feature "Community Events" columns. Before you do, call the publication to see what its deadlines are to make sure your release arrives in time. Send the release to all the media and to the daybook editors of the wire services. There should be a regional office of the Associated Press or United Press International in your area (see Chapter 3).

Some publications may simply list your event; others may run a short article about upcoming events. Study your local media. Community service events, as well as ceremonies, have a good chance of being covered as local news. Again, check with the individual publication concerning its policies.

Will preevent publicity bring in a crowd? That's difficult to say. It depends on the publication as well as the type of coverage. A feature article will attract more people than an "events" listing, for example. You can research this by talking to others who have had events listed in the publications.

These are just a few ways for you to create opportunities for public involvement and promote that involvement through the media at minimal cost. The rewards to your organization will be greater than the attention garnered in the media. Through these experiences, you can build alliances within various communities, and those relationships can provide benefits to everyone involved.

Presentations

Platform presentations and speeches are an indispensable community public relations tool.

These occasions offer an opportunity to let your personality, as well as your expertise, shine through. Whether you're speaking before a crowd of 5000 or a group of 30 school children, or just doing a one-on-one interview, it's important that you exhibit enthusiasm, energy, and excitement. If you want people to believe the message you're trying to get across, you have to let them see, hear, and, most important, feel what you feel.

Nonetheless, almost all of us wish that we had better presentation skills. Most people also wish they had greater self-confidence. Even when we give presentations regularly, it can be uncomfortable. In fact, it is said that the fear of public speaking ranks right up there beside other major life crises, such as loss of a job, divorce, illness, and even death itself.

By following some simple guidelines, you can increase your comfort level and the effectiveness of your message.

First, know the audience. The coordinator of the event should be able to fill you in on your audience's level of knowledge about the topic, the type of information they need and want, and whether they expect to be instructed, informed, motivated, or persuaded.

Next, determine the objectives of your message. Ask yourself, "What points do I want my audience to carry home and remember?" Your objectives should be related to your audience's needs and should be stated in terms of what you want the audience members to remember when they leave the room and what you'd like them to be able to do as a result of having listened to you.

Choose slides carefully. Used effectively, they can be a great addition to a presentation. Do not hide behind the slides, however, by focusing solely on your visual aids. The darkened room may invite too many people to doze off!

Rehearse your speech carefully. Make sure it is the appropriate length. Twenty minutes is probably the maximum. If possible, practice the speech before a group of colleagues or your family and ask for feedback concerning timing, delivery, and content.

Make it as easy as possible for the audience. Begin with a joke or anecdote—provided that it is truly funny and appropriate for the occasion. Thank your host, then state briefly what you're hoping to accomplish.

Use invigorating language. Remember, you are talking to the public, not a scholarly audience. For example, say, "Let's take a look at this!" rather than "Now, if you'll notice on the left-hand side of your screen, we have a slide that depicts..." When needed, clarify a point by saying, "I can easily understand how looking at that graphic, you might have thought that. Let's put the graphic back on and take a new look."

TOP TIPS

Planning Effective Presentations

Your presentation should stimulate thought and carry across your data and ideas. While planning, you should:

Limit content to a few important points.

Use information that is accurate and up to date.

Rehearse carefully out loud to fit the allotted time. Visualize the setting and your audience, and practice using gestures.

Coordinate your commentary with appropriate use of slides or audio-visual aids.

Repeat Presentations: Building on Success

A single presentation cannot be expected to realize optimum results. Repetition is the name of the game. It may take six presentations before the momentum builds and word-of-mouth spreads to pull in hesitant potential attendees who don't want to spend their time on anything unless they believe they can benefit.

If you practice in a hospital, nursing facility, or HMO, giving a program will bring you out where the community can get to know and respect you personally. Many hospital pharmacists find the direct patient contact inspiring and instructive.

And consider the impact your involvement in such presentations can have on your stature at work. You may well find your hospital willing to fund the program and projection equipment, in return for your willingness to generate goodwill through the presentations.

Presentation Topics

Topics can be right out of the news such as legislation affecting drug use or new drug treatments. Possible "stump speech" topics follow.

Using Medicines "On Hand"

A child becomes ill. Mother looks into the medicine cabinet to find a remedy. There may be a partial prescription, one that has expired. Consumers don't always understand that many prescriptions should be taken in full. Also, they need to be informed that someone else's prescription should never be used, because similar symptoms do not automatically mean the same dosage is the right dosage, or even the right medication.

Drug Interactions

Many patients are not aware of potential interactions that can negate the effectiveness of the prescription, nor do they realize that some interactions may be fatal.

Interpreting the Instructions

What does "Take four times daily with lots of water" mean? What may seem clear to a pharmacist may be very ambiguous to a patient.

Proper Drug Use

From time to time, the media focus public attention on some form of drug abuse with a media blitz. When that happens, it is especially timely to propose programs on the proper use of drugs.

Health Fairs

Health fairs are an important means of familiarizing the community with the various services you provide and helping your patients acquire needed self-help skills. A fair consists of information booths set up by various health education services. Health fairs provide an excellent opportunity for collaboration between pharmacists, physicians, and other community healthcare professionals. They also offer chances for cooperating with disease-specific societies such as the local chapters of the United Way, March of Dimes, American Cancer Society, and American Heart Association. These and various other organizations can provide a wide variety of topics and educational materials.

Planning a health fair is like planning a big party. The more people you get involved, the easier, more enjoyable, and more successful it will be.

Organizing a Health Fair

Organizing a health fair need not be expensive. Each of the involved organizations should be responsible for its own display and handouts. If you are the main sponsor, your primary responsibility would be to get as many people involved and excited about this project as possible.

Date. Schedule your event when there are not a lot of competing public gatherings. Check with City Hall to see if any permits have been issued for that day. Check with any community calendars in your area.

When selecting the date for a health fair, also consider the impact it will have on your staff. Health fairs on Thursdays or Fridays are usually more successful, because people are already in a weekend mood; however, fairs should not be held on the days preceding holiday weekends.

Time. Your health fair could last between two and six hours. The most popular times are between 11:00 a.m. and 3:00 p.m. Other factors you may wish to consider include:

- Will it conflict with other important meetings, conferences, or other events?
- Will it interfere with any special work projects, deadlines, or staff vacation schedules?
- What time frame will be most convenient for the majority of your staff? (This factor is especially important if you have multiple shifts.)
- What is the best available facility open that particular day and time?

Making Effective Presentations

TOP TIPS

Keep eye contact. It makes people feel connected to you.

Maintain good posture.

Use gestures. They can help you paint pictures with words, but make sure they don't get in the way.

Be enthusiastic. If you don't care, why should they?

Speak clearly and use proper language. Do not use slang, jargon, or technical terms.

Breathe. It helps you control your nervousness and also gives you time to gather your thoughts.

Modulate your voice. The tone of your voice can create or change a mood.

Dress conservatively. Be neat and professional. Don't wear loud accessories that will distract the audience.

Smile! It will not only make you look and feel better but also will make your audience more receptive.

Location and Organization. Selecting a central, easily accessible location for the health fair will attract many more people than if you hold it in a more remote location.

You need to consider the floor plan and physical space requirements, booth placement, traffic flow, lighting and outlet considerations, table and chair requirements and placement, and more, to make the event a success.

Promoting the Health Fair

Good promotion is critical to the success of any health fair. Here are some ideas.

Place articles about the fair in your newsletter. If a newsletter is distributed monthly, an announcement the month before and the month of the health fair is recommended.

Produce and distribute promotional materials such as flyers and posters and post them throughout the neighborhood.

Additional materials to enhance the success of your health fair may include balloons, crepe paper, signs, and posters; raffle prizes such as lunch for two, health club memberships, movie passes, tickets to local attractions, hats, logo T-shirts, and other donated articles; and healthful foods and snacks.

Make sure you allocate enough time to prepare for your event.

Communicating with the Community in Writing

A newsletter is useful when you want to communicate several different kinds of information at one time and on a regular basis. A newspaper column is another effective way to communicate regularly with the community.

Pharmacy Newsletters

The purpose of the newsletter should be to educate and update your constituents or patients. By picking a specific topic such as what is happening on important health issues, you will establish the focus of the newsletter.

The newsletter can be weekly, monthly, or quarterly based upon the amount of information you have to convey and the amount of time you are going to devote to it. It need not be complicated or long—two to four typewritten pages are standard. It can be produced very inexpensively by using 8½" × 11" paper and the computer you have at your pharmacy. Design and layout are as important as the written copy. Use a creative name and headline or colored or bold headlines to catch the reader's eye.

If you wish, divide the newsletter into several columns that will be regular features. These columns provide a format to follow each time and to allow your readers to become familiar with the newsletter.

To keep the tone of the newsletter consistent and ensure that there are no contradictory or duplicate messages, one person should edit it. You may ask staff or others to contribute articles or serve as correspondents who can report to you on the happenings of their departments. However, you should reserve the right to edit as necessary.

Newspaper Columns

One effective way to enhance your professional standing among your current and prospective patients is to write a newspaper column. Health is a subject of much interest, and if your local paper has no such column, the editor likely will respond favorably to your inquiry.

If you have some doubts about your writing skills, the best format might be a "question and answer" style. As starters, consider the questions asked most frequently in your pharmacy. State the question and give your answer.

Type three sample columns and approach the feature editor of your newspaper. You can save yourself some pressure by always staying two columns ahead, thus avoiding a time crunch in meeting deadlines.

Summary

There's no better way to be noticed by your publics, and be noticed in the best possible light, than by performing a service. Whether it's participating in a community health screening or working with the schools, public service makes you a part of the community, builds visibility and trust, and cements your relationship with the very people with whom you want to do business. This is the essence of public relations.◗

Celebrating National Health Observances

One of your most important responsibilities is assuring patients that you have their best interests in mind. A good way to let them see this, as well as to create positive public relations for pharmacy, is to become involved in national health observances. For pharmacists, two of the most important of these occasions are National Pharmacy Week, which is observed the last week in October, and National Poison Prevention Week, observed every March. There are, however, countless other national events in which you may participate.

This chapter describes how pharmacists can take an active role in community celebrations of these national events. It presents detailed information on planning and staffing telephone hotlines. Hotlines may be tied in with a national health observance and are a visible and rewarding way to get involved with the community.

Opportunities for Health Observances

Health observances are days, weeks, or months devoted to promoting awareness of particular health concerns. These events are generally initiated at the national level and carried out in local communities nationwide.

Health professionals, community groups, and others can use these nationally supported events to sponsor health promotion events, stimulate awareness of health risks, or focus on disease prevention. Materials available from sponsoring organizations range from a simple flyer to sophisticated packets of promotional materials that include posters, videos, buttons, balloons, and even T-shirts.

The accompanying box lists some of the major national events in which you may want to take part.

You don't have to celebrate an event every month, desirable though that might be. You can get a great boost just by participating in two or three a year. Choose those that your staff is best suited for and that are of greatest interest to your patient population.

National Health Observances

January	March of Dimes Birth Defects Prevention Month
	National Eye Care Month
	National Glaucoma Awareness Month
	National Thyroid Awareness Month
February	American Heart Month
	Sinus Pain Awareness Month
	Wise Health Consumer Month
March	National Chronic Fatigue Syndrome
	Awareness Month
	National Kidney Month
	National Nutrition Month
	Workplace Eye Health and Safety Month
April	Child Abuse Prevention Month
	National Occupational Therapy Month
	National Sexually Transmitted Diseases
	Awareness Month
	Women's Eye Health and Safety Month
May	Allergy and Asthma Awareness Month
	Better Sleep Month
	Breathe Easy Month
	Hepatitis Awareness Month
	Huntington's Disease Awareness Month
	Medic Alert Awareness Month
	National Arthritis Month
	National Digestive Diseases Awareness Month
	National High Blood Pressure Month
	National Osteoporosis Prevention Month
	National Sight-Saving Month
	National Stroke Awareness Month
	Older Americans Month
June	National Safety Month
	Vision Research Month
	Fireworks Safety Month

July	Hemochromatosis Screening Awareness Month
August	National Spinal Muscular Atrophy Awareness Month
September	Baby Safety Month Children's Eye Health and Safety Month Gynecologic Cancer Awareness Month Healthy Aging Month Leukemia Awareness Month National Cholesterol Education Month National Pediculosis Prevention Month
October	Child Health Month Healthy Lung Month Liver Awareness Month Lupus Awareness Month March of Dimes Campaign for Healthier Babies National Breast Cancer Awareness Month National Dental Hygiene Month National Family Health Month Talk About Prescriptions Month National Pharmacy Week
November	American Diabetes Month Diabetic Eye Disease Awareness Month Epilepsy Awareness Month National Alzheimer's Disease Month National Hospice Month
December	Jingle Bell Run for Arthritis Safe Toys and Gifts

Check the Web sites of the sponsoring organizations for more information on these events.

For example, the National Heart, Lung, and Blood Institute sponsors a National Cholesterol Education Program in September. This program is a prime opportunity for a pharmacist to set up a cholesterol-testing machine or to counsel patients on how to lower cholesterol levels through proper diet and use of medications.

Target your participation to the needs of your own patient population. For example, if you have a predominantly young population, you may want to focus on Child Abuse Prevention Month. If you have a great number of older citizens, you may want to participate in activities conducted in association with National Alzheimer's Disease Month.

Contact the organization leaders sponsoring the activity and inform them that you are interested in helping. They will provide an information kit filled with ideas, useful media tips, and order forms for materials. These materials may be free; if not, the charge is minimal.

If you decide to take part in such a campaign, send news releases and public service announcements to your local media describing the service you are providing to your patients. As described in the information on news releases and media alerts (see Chapter 4), remember to let them know the "who, what, when, where, and why" of the event.

You can also inform the public by making personal contact at your practice site or in hospitals, nursing homes, businesses, and schools, and with elected officials.

Events and Activities

How will you celebrate a national health observance within your pharmacy? Every part of our nation is different; therefore you may have unique celebration ideas for your local community. Be creative and open to providing a wide range of activities.

One of the most popular ways to celebrate a national event is to hold a health fair (see Chapter 7). These events, which are often jointly sponsored by a number of local organizations, are a great means of attracting public attention and providing a valuable service. A description of a successful health fair sponsored by the School of Pharmacy at the University of Buffalo appears in Chapter 9.

Other ideas include the following:

▶ Make a special phone message promoting the observance. Use it when you answer the phone and tape record it so that it runs when the line is busy or the pharmacy is closed.

▶ Organize a "brown bag" medicine review program in your community. Invite patients to bring all their medicines in a bag and discuss them with their pharmacist. Patients are advised if medicines are out of date, and which medicines, if used in combination incorrectly, can cause harmful interactions.

▶ Create radio public service announcements (PSAs) and distribute them to radio stations in your community (see Chapter 4). Each of the PSAs can be "tagged" with your practice site name as a cosponsor, creating visibility for your practice.

▶ Contact local television health reporters. Ask them to air stories about the observance you have chosen to celebrate. Offer to be an on-air expert.

▶ Organize a medicine information and education display in local libraries and at your own practice site.

▶ Visit classrooms, nursing homes, senior centers, and other community sites. Consumers of all ages benefit from discussions about how to use medicines safely and effectively.

Celebrating a National Health Observance in Hospitals and Institutional Settings

National health observances are often celebrated in hospitals and health systems. Spread the word in your organization's newsletter. Include information about what pharmacists do and how they help patients with their drug therapy regimens.

Extend your gratitude with an Appreciation Day. Organize one of these events to show appreciation for people who use your facilities. If you work in a hospital, develop a list of patient contacts. Use the list to invite people to the event ("brown bag" lunch, potluck dinner, or hospital-sponsored meal). Introduce medication services that are available to them through your hospital.

If you work in a long-term-care facility, consider holding an information program for residents and/or their families. The program can explain the role of the pharmacist in disease state management and the role of your facility in patient care; if possible, you can include the launch of an ongoing program for residents.

Partner with senior programs. Many hospitals and long-term-care facilities already have programs for older people. Find ways to tap into these programs and include pharmacy information in the programs that they offer. Have brochures available for distribution.

Hold an open house at the facility and invite all employees to visit the pharmacy. Serve refreshments and hold a drawing or contest offering gift certificates to an area restaurant.

Ideas for Pharmacy Students

The Friday of National Pharmacy Week has been designated as National Pharmacy Student Day. This day is a good one for pharmacy students to get out into the community and work with the public to promote pharmacy. This day would also be a good time for colleges to open their doors and educate the public about pharmacy programs. This step would work not only as a recruiting technique but also as a means of educating the public about the challenging nature of the pharmacy curriculum.

Team up with a local or state pharmacy association to promote the value of pharmacy services. Any of the national observances listed earlier in this chapter might be adapted for such joint efforts.

Talk to local high school students about careers in pharmacy.

Write an article for the college newspaper about an important health issue, such as drug interactions or drug abuse.

If you work part-time in a pharmacy, take the initiative to help your supervisor plan activities for the national health observance.

Telephone Hotlines

Telephone hotlines are popping up everywhere these days. They combine public service and public relations in a way that makes the sponsoring organization look good and conveys much needed health information to a concerned public. A particularly effective time to sponsor a phone hotline would be in conjunction with the observance of a national health week such as Poison Prevention Week, Immunization Awareness Month, Talk About Prescriptions Month, or National Pharmacy Week.

If you're interested in pursuing this idea, ask your colleagues whether they would be interested in staffing a telephone hotline and responding to specific questions from the public on drug therapy issues. If they agree, approach a local newspaper or TV station and ask them to sponsor the hotline by providing facilities and phone lines. The newspaper or TV station can also feature stories promoting the hotline to the public and offer on-the-spot and follow-up coverage of the event. Organizing a hotline requires at least two months of planning, but it is a terrific way to reach a large audience.

Hosting a Hotline

Local hotlines require relatively modest resources in terms of funding and volunteers, but they do require careful preparation and organization. Planning and conducting a hotline entails the following activities.

Choosing a Message

What topics are you qualified to address that would be of interest to the public? Possible topics include drug information, medication errors, disease state management, and how to stock your medicine cabinet.

Your hotline will get more attention if it has a distinctive logo or slogan. Posters and brochures that incorporate the hotline number are also helpful.

Your theme should be used on all hotline materials and news releases and in decorations at the hotline site. If you are holding your event in conjunction with a national celebration sponsored by a health organization, you may use its materials. Creating your own materials, another option, is more expensive but has the advantage of being more tailored to your specific event or cause. If your budget permits, you may want to use the theme on T-shirts and lapel stickers for the volunteers.

Finding an Event Coordinator

Is there an individual willing to take charge of the hotline, including recruiting and scheduling of volunteers? This position must be assumed by a capable, personable individual who has the time to devote to a very intensive activity.

Finding a Suitable Location

You'll need a suitable location—a spacious, comfortable room where a number of phones can be installed. The room should be large enough to set up long tables with no more than one or two phones on each. The volunteers should not be seated so close to each other that they have difficulty hearing and making themselves heard to hotline callers. There should be a separate sign-in table with a nonhotline phone for coordinators. Arrange to have a table with refreshments in a corner of the room or in a nearby area where the volunteers can relax during breaks or after their shifts.

Timing

You'll also need to decide on hours. Should the hotline operate during the day, or should you make it more accessible to working pharmacists by opening the lines in the late afternoon and evening? These are the questions you must answer.

Recruiting Volunteers

You will need knowledgeable volunteers to staff your hotline. Do you have enough qualified people with the time and willingness to serve on a hotline? Can you count on their participation? You need to recruit your volunteers well in advance with a definite time slot and remind them at least twice of their commitment.

Determine the number of volunteers you will need by multiplying the number of lines by the number of shifts needed to cover the hotline hours—plus a few extra to fill in for "no shows." Each volunteer should be asked to work a 2–3-hour shift, a period long enough to answer a variety of calls, but short enough to avoid weariness. You may also want volunteers to help with hotline administration and publicity.

Begin recruiting volunteers as early as possible. As volunteers respond, assign them to specific times on a master list of hotline shifts. Follow up immediately with a confirmation note that describes what is expected of them and describes any materials you feel would be useful. Be sure to provide telephone numbers that the volunteers can call in case schedule changes are necessary.

A few days before the event, send the volunteers reminders of their assigned shifts and the hotline location, with a request to check in about 15 minutes early.

Costs of a Hotline

Hotline costs can vary considerably, depending on the number and location of phone lines. Phone costs will be your single greatest expense. You will need to obtain a special toll-free or local phone number, buy or rent telephones, and arrange to have them installed so that they ring in sequence instead of simultaneously.

Other expenses may include postage and telephone costs incurred in recruiting volunteers, room rental, refreshments for volunteers, publicity costs (printing, postage, banners), travel expenses, meals, and incidentals (name tags, certificates of appreciation, T-shirts or other novelty items).

You may be able to persuade a local business or corporation to fund your hotline as a public service. (The local phone company would be an obvious candidate!) You might try approaching a local TV or radio station about cosponsoring the hotline in connection with an event like National Pharmacy Week. It would draw a large audience, and you would certainly get more calls.

Promoting the Hotline

The secret of a successful hotline is to select a timely topic and make sure that people know about it and have the number handy. That takes a good deal of publicity.

Do you have a good relationship with your local newspaper and radio or TV station? Take advantage of it to build interest in the hotline and to publicize the hotline number. (Remember, of course, that if you've succeeded in getting a local television station to serve as a place to hold the hotline, its competitors may decide not to publicize the event.)

Send a news release describing the hotline to newspapers and radio stations at least two weeks before the event. Offer to arrange for hotline volunteers to be interviewed by TV, radio, and newspaper reporters before or during the event.

Don't depend exclusively on the media. Be prepared to promote the hotline to the local community. Publicize the hotline in your own practice site. In addition, furnish each volunteer with multiple copies of personalized news releases with the headline, "Local Pharmacist to Participate in Medication

Hotline." The pharmacist/volunteer can forward these to his or her local newspapers, radio stations, and other publications.

During the Hotline

As volunteers arrive for their assigned shifts, they should sign in and be greeted by the hotline coordinator. They should be briefed on how to answer each call (for example, "This is the Pharmacy Hotline. My name is John Smith, Registered Pharmacist. How can I help you?"). They should also be given a script for what to say when they don't know the answer (for example, "If you'll give me your name and telephone number, I'll see to it that you receive this information"), and a suggested time limit for calls (usually 10 minutes).

If a volunteer cannot answer a question, he or she should record the question with the name and number of the caller. Have someone call back during the hotline operation or as soon as possible afterwards.

Each volunteer should have a log sheet on which to record the number of calls answered, as well as such useful information as the topics discussed and the type of caller. Collect the log sheets when the volunteers leave, and use them later to analyze and evaluate the hotline.

Possible Problems

If you're just beginning, you may have some minor problems. Experienced hotline organizers have noted, for example, the following possible glitches.

Telephone malfunctions. The coordinator should have emergency numbers to call if a technician is needed, but remember that most telephone companies won't send anyone on weekends.

"No shows." Be sure you have some stand-by volunteers on hand—or know where they can be reached quickly. Otherwise, you either have to ask a volunteer to take an extra shift or unplug a phone.

Crank calls. Some callers may be difficult to deal with. Alert your volunteers to be polite, excuse themselves, and simply hang up.

Noise and congestion. Noise can be especially bothersome during shift-changing times. The problem can be minimized by efficient check-in and check-out procedures and by limiting the number of "outsiders" such as friends and family members of volunteers at the hotline site.

Lack of calls. If the number of calls is disappointing, try to determine the reason: Insufficient publicity? Boring topic? Lack of public interest? Bad timing? Be better prepared next time.

Follow-Up Activities

There are some follow-up steps that you should take once the hotline's time is up, the phones are silent, and the last volunteers have departed.

- Be sure you have disconnected the phones and arranged to have them removed and the hotline number discontinued. Failure to take these steps promptly may incur additional charges.
- Send thank-you letters to the sponsors, coordinators, volunteers, and everyone else who helped make the hotline a success. You might also print a recognition certificate that the recipients can frame and display.

PERSONAL EXAMPLE

Hotline No. 1

The first hotline I ever coordinated was with *USA Today*. Pharmacists staffed the hotline, and consumers could call in.

On the day the hotline was scheduled, a major drug manufacturer was involved in a scandal concerning generic drugs. It was on the front page of every newspaper in the country. *USA Today* took advantage of the breaking news and added this highlight to its promotional copy about the hotline—"Confused about the safety and effectiveness of generic and brand-name drugs?"

A full-page series of articles appeared in that publication on the day of the hotline featuring subjects such as, "Pharmacists' top job: Filling in customers," "Stocking your medicine chest," and "Over-the-counter considerations," along with the national 800 number.

The pharmacist volunteers, who were recruited from the Washington, D.C., area, were scheduled to work in 3-hour shifts from 9:00 a.m. to 9:00 p.m. During the 12-hour hotline, they answered more than 2000 calls from consumers around the country. Many calls were from consumers concerned about the quality of their generic drugs.

A reporter from *USA Today* was assigned to cover the event. The pharmacist hotline received coverage in that publication on the day before, the day of, and the day after the event. The paper devoted hundreds of thousands of dollars' worth of space to the promotion of this event.

The preparations for the event were time consuming. They included recruiting and training the pharmacists, preparing a briefing book, and managing a host of other details. Nonetheless, it was well worth the effort.

▶ Check the log sheets to determine how many calls were recorded, the nature of the calls, the categories of callers, and other useful data. You may also want to meet with some of the volunteers to discuss and evaluate the hotline.

▶ Send a news release summarizing the results to the local media.

▶ Review your hotline experience while it is still fresh. Note things that could be changed or improved next time. Did you have too few or too many phones? Should you include bilingual volunteers to answer questions of callers whose English is limited?

▶ Keep the names and telephone numbers of the volunteers on file for future use.

Summary

Pharmacists can tap into well-established national health observances to build community goodwill and promote public health. They may celebrate the events using materials they have obtained from a national sponsor or develop their own. Telephone hotlines are an especially effective activity to hold in conjunction with a national health observance.▶

How Pharmacy Students Can Use Public Relations

While pharmacy students may find the information contained throughout this book useful, there are some ideas that apply specifically to their needs. I spent some time polling pharmacy student leaders and interviewing students about what they would find useful in conducting a public relations program on campus. This chapter summarizes my findings and contains some ideas that you may want to try.

What Can Students Do?

If you're a student, you can go into the community to create a greater awareness of the profession. You can work with pharmacists in local practice settings to set up health fairs, screenings, and other patient education programs.

Another strategy is to work with the public relations or public information officers at your school or college of pharmacy. If you can relate the importance of what you are doing—whether it's a series of "brown bag" events or a poison prevention effort to a member of the public relations office and let that person know the impact of the activity, they will probably be interested in getting involved. Their experience, know-how, and community contacts could be crucial to the success of your efforts. In approaching the office, be prepared with statistics on such timely matters as how many people don't take their medications correctly or how many people were hospitalized in the past month or year for drug interactions because they did not know how to properly take their medications.

Determining Your Needs

If you are interested in mounting a public relations program of any sort, begin by assessing your resources. At the beginning of the year, meet with your fellow chapter officers to discuss your resources and needs. How much money do you have? How much will you need? How soon do you need it?

On the basis of your answers to these questions, decide which activities should be sponsored during the year. List each project that your chapter plans to sponsor and itemize each expense involved in the projects to the best of your ability. Overestimate any expenses of which you are not sure. For each activity, also list the sources of income that will be used to pay for that project.

Try to maintain a balance between realism and daring. Don't be afraid of having grand goals; just be sure to set priorities from the start according to how much you can afford to spend. Leave some room for unexpected costs.

Also be aware that public relations takes long-term planning. If you're just starting out and want to do a big event, you might even want to plan a full academic year ahead. More modest events can be undertaken in a much shorter period.

Finally, be realistic. Evaluate how much money you will need for a project before you begin raising money. Such planning allows you extra control over your income and expenses. It also makes you look like a professional fundraiser when approaching administrators and outside funding sources. Have a backup plan if a funding source doesn't come through.

Finding Funds

Once you have assessed your resources and identified your needs, it's time to start looking for funds and support. What are your options?

Begin by asking your dean or department head for funding. One of the secrets of fundraising is to find someone who shares your objectives and values. For that reason alone, starting in your department is a good idea.

Then branch out. Think about potential sources for money and for services and in-kind support. Ask local printers to donate photocopying and paper, and ask store owners for merchandise for a raffle. Look in your area for pharmaceutical companies, health maintenance organizations (HMOs), and corporate foundations willing to sponsor your activities.

You need to develop a list of prospective donors—people who are interested in what you are doing. Then get them excited about what you are doing and if possible get them involved.

Look for substantial supporters. Look toward philanthropic organizations (e.g., the American Red Cross) for fundraising assistance. Your local library has books that list state and local foundations and also describe their individual giving histories and request requirements.

Some are other possible sources of funding are national corporations; local foundations; pharmaceutical, insurance, and medical supply companies; HMOs and local businesses; and grant programs.

"Friend Raising"

A good way to develop your initial list is to hold a special event. Special events are for "friend raising," not fundraising. At this event, have several door prizes donated by local businesses that you will publicly acknowledge at least once. Invite those who attend to sign up for the door prizes.

Once your event has been successfully carried out, send a thank-you note, including a photo from the event the sponsor helped to fund. It establishes a good rapport between your chapter and your sponsors. This acknowledgment will help you next year when you are seeking funding.

Now put the list of those who have attended your event to use. The people that you now have on your list are at least somewhat interested in your cause because they showed up for the event. They also know something about your school.

Within three days, mail a letter to everyone on the list. Thank them for coming. Tell them a moving story about how your school is helping someone in the community, and how it is only possible with the support of good people like them. In that letter, ask for a contribution. Include a return envelope to make it easy for the donor. Convenience should be an important consideration in anything you do. Start working on that letter about two months before the event, so that it's done in time.

Follow up with a phone call. To ensure that your letter doesn't end up at the bottom of the pile, send another letter making a final pitch.

Formalize your project plans before asking for money. This process establishes credibility and justifies your needs. Have a reasonable budget, objectives, and a realistic plan of action to present on paper. A clear and professional presentation may give you a winning edge.

Finally, it's essential to plan ahead. Many grant-giving organizations have limited funds and award them on an annual basis. Donations must be solicited months in advance of when you expect to use the money, and close follow-up is necessary.

Writing Fundraising Letters

Keep in mind that whenever you are asking for money that you are providing a service. Tell people what you've done and what you plan to do to achieve progress and success. Longer letters appear to do better because you can address all concerns and potential concerns. Make the letter compelling. Use short paragraphs (no more than three sentences) or bulleted items.

Always start the letter with a series of good news items to build momentum and make the entire letter entertaining and informative. Describe what you want to do, why you're going to do it, how you're going to do it, and what results you expect.

Sample Fundraising Letter

Date

Name
Address
City/State/Zip

Dear Mr. Smith:

This year's observance of National Pharmacy Week is scheduled for the last full week of October, and promotional activities have already begun. This year's theme is "Educate Before You Medicate—Talk With Your Pharmacist." We are currently planning a Health Fair in our community, and we invite you to participate in this promotion.

Interest in National Pharmacy Week continues to grow each year, and one of the key elements of the program has been these student-sponsored Health Fairs. Last year, we worked with hundreds of patients in conjunction with Smith's Pharmacy to inform them of the valuable role pharmacists play in the management of their health.

Our feedback from patients indicates that they look forward to these Health Fairs each year, and each year the volume of consumers continues to increase. The media have also become involved in this annual promotion. Our local radio station has done a live remote from the site of the Health Fair, interviewing patients throughout the day.

This year, we would like to invite your organization to become a sponsor of this event. You can participate by providing us with an educational grant in the amount of $[fill in] or by donating patient brochures [or products, instruments, etc.].

We would like to include your organization as a sponsor on the program materials as well as in the media materials that will be sent out, so we would appreciate your commitment by [insert date].

I will call you in a few days to discuss your participation, but feel free to call me at (000) 000-0000 with any questions. I hope we can make this program even more successful than ever. I look forward to speaking with you soon.

Sincerely,

Your Name

Fundraising Events

Get your imagination involved to come up with a unique event or unique slant. Some successful events have included health fairs, auctions, and raffles, but see if you can find ways to tailor events to your community.

Health Fairs

Pharmaceutical and medical supply companies, pharmacy textbook publishers, and others lease booths or tables at student-planned health fairs. Approach any companies who want to advertise to the pharmacy school community. Each company can be charged from $100 to $350 per table.

Some companies may donate books in addition to their registration fee, and these items can be sold or raffled. Your health fair can be a free-standing event or part of a larger event. See Chapter 7 for more details.

Auctions

Invite students, parents, community members, and faculty for an evening of light food, beverages, and an auction. The idea is to get everything donated by local merchants and restaurants in exchange for recognition as a sponsor in the auction brochure. Solicit participation from gift shops, department stores, florists, restaurants, printers, hotels, record shops, and galleries. People might be more willing to donate if part of your profits go to a worthy local charity, like a women's shelter. Ask a local caterer to donate food; ask a wine merchant to provide wine.

Raffles

Raffles are simpler than auctions. Solicit items in the same manner as for an auction, but issue raffle tickets instead of conducting an auction. Display the items, and sell tickets for a fixed price. Then randomly select winners for each prize.

Public Service Campaigns

Another idea for pharmacy students is to conduct a local public service campaign. Here's an example of one such effort conducted by pharmacy students at the University of North Carolina.

As part of their course on nonprescription drugs, the students at the University of North Carolina School of Pharmacy were asked to prepare radio public service announcements (PSAs) that could compliment a national public relations initiative of the American Pharmaceutical Association. Here are some examples of the PSAs the students created to promote the expertise of the pharmacist. You may want to adapt them for your own specific campaigns.

10-Second PSAs

▶ Pharmacists can play an important role in your healthcare. Use your pharmacist to obtain essential information about your prescriptions and over-the-counter products.

▶ Take control of your health! A variety of health problems can be treated safely with nonprescription therapies. Your pharmacist can help you chose the therapy that is right for you!

▶ Your pharmacist is a valuable resource who can provide you with answers regarding nonprescription medications. [YOUR PHARMACY] encourages you to read the product label, know the benefits and risks of what you are taking, and always talk to your pharmacist if you have questions.

30-Second PSAs

▶ Are you using any herbal products? If so, have you talked with your pharmacist to discuss possible drug interactions? Many herbal products interact with prescription or over-the-counter drug products. For example, ginseng interferes with a commonly used blood-thinning agent as well as with estrogen replacement therapy. Aloe may interfere with certain blood pressure medications. Don't let yourself fall victim to one of these interactions. Talk to your pharmacist today to determine which herbal products are safe for you!

▶ How many nonprescription medications do you have in your medicine cabinet right now? Probably quite a few. But how many times did you consult with your pharmacist before buying one? Over-the-counter medications can have side effects, drug interactions, and special instructions for use just like drugs that require a prescription. A pharmacist is a knowledgeable and accessible healthcare professional who can answer your questions about all medications to help you stay healthy. So don't forget to ask your pharmacist if the medicine you have chosen is the right medicine for you.

Conducting a PSA campaign can be a good way to become involved with your local media. See Chapter 4 for details on how to place PSAs.

Fundraising Needs Publicity

Trying to raise funds without publicity is like trying to sail without wind. If people don't know you're trying to raise funds—or if they've never heard of you or your cause—you're operating under a tremendous handicap. If you expect anyone to support you, then you must tell them who you are, what you have to offer, what you're doing, what you've done, what you hope to do in the future.

Publicity alone won't convince anyone to support a cause he or she doesn't believe in. It is only a vehicle you can use to carry your story and your sales pitch to everyone within your community. Nonetheless, it is hard to overestimate its value.

How do you tell them? With publicity.

Media Coverage

Media coverage, as described elsewhere in this book, includes, among other things, hard and "soft" news stories in local and national papers, stories in consumer and trade magazines, and radio and TV appearances. The more positive media coverage you secure, the better.

Unfortunately, beginners often feel that a few news articles in the local paper during fundraising time are all that's needed and all they can expect to get. They don't realize the value of a year-round publicity campaign. Why? Because continuing notice in the media raises public awareness of your school, because it shows that independent sources consider your activities newsworthy, and because it gives your group credibility.

As a result of this publicity, your past contributors will take pride in having supported you and will be inclined to do it again. And, when you approach potential contributors, your job will be half done. The public will know who you are and what you do. They'll understand the importance of your work.

Being Your Own Media Agent

Media publicity is crucial because it gives you credibility. But it's not the only publicity outlet available to you. You can also create your own publicity, without newspapers or radio or television. T-shirts can get the name of your school or event out in public, and, of course, you can sell them to raise money.

You can put up posters in store windows, bank windows, restaurants, or other places where the public is likely to see them. Create displays in stores or demonstrations that bring attention to the work your school does. You can put flyers on car windshields. You can organize a word-of-mouth campaign.

Request space for your posters where the people you most want to reach are likely to see them. Window displays create a public awareness of your school or an event that's coming up. The topic of the displays can be practically anything that is of sufficiently broad interest.

Visiting community gathering places and talking with merchants and business people is, in and of itself, good publicity. It puts people from your organization into contact with others in the community. In addition to publicizing a particular event, posters are good for spreading the institutional message and letting the public know that you exist and that you offer services that may be of value to them. So, don't be discouraged. Even if your requests for space are turned down, you will have a chance to talk about your organization and find out how much business people know about it and what their impression is.

When it comes to creating the posters or displays, be resourceful. If there is an artist in your community who will volunteer to design a poster for you, then the offer of a design, and the unveiling, are good for publicity. If there is no celebrity artist available to you, then the local art teacher or a college student might volunteer.

You could even sponsor a contest for a poster design. The contest itself becomes the occasion for more publicity, as you announce the contest and the judges, choose the winner, and present an award.

Another valuable promotional tool you can use year-round is a newsletter that goes to your constituencies—whomever you want to keep informed of your activities.

CASE STUDY: Fundraising at the University of Buffalo School of Pharmacy

In anticipation of National Pharmacy Week, the University of Buffalo School of Pharmacy, along with others, sponsored a Pharmacy Health and Wellness Fair from 11:00 a.m. to 3:00 p.m. on the campus.

Pharmacists and pharmacy student volunteers worked to educate the public on various subjects. There were booths specifically for the patient management of:

- Asthma—Pharmacists staffing this booth gave out patient information and had demo inhalers and peak flow meters to help patients understand this disease (avoidance of triggers, proper inhaler usage, signs of serious problems).

- Cholesterol—Pharmacists and nurses gave out patient literature educating the patient about the dangers of high cholesterol. Patients were able to have their cholesterol checked.

- Blood Pressure—Patients were able to have their blood pressure taken, patient literature was handed out, medication questions were answered, and the importance of adherence was addressed.

- Diabetes—Pharmacists and nurses checked blood glucose levels for patients who requested it and interacted with patients regarding insulin and medication use, proper skin care, and diet.

There was also:

- A Drug Information Booth where patient literature was available.

- A Brown Bag Area where patients could bring in their medications and interact with pharmacists on an informal basis. Patients were able to discuss their therapy with pharmacists and pharmacy students and ask questions about health-related issues.

▶ A Poison Prevention Booth that highlighted the large Poison Prevention Awareness Program of the School of Pharmacy and the Western New York Poison Control Center. This program has educated thousands of western New York families and their elementary age children in the Buffalo area in one year; it ran during National Poison Prevention Week in March.

Another example of a successful effort of getting your name in front of people to aid in fundraising and to do something worthwhile at the same time is *Operation Immunization*. This national immunization awareness program is designed and implemented by pharmacy students. The goal of the program is to make communities more aware of immunizations and the role of the pharmacist.

CASE STUDY: How Pharmacy Students Made Operation Immunization a Success

Background

Each year, at least 60,000 Americans die of vaccine-preventable diseases. While a great deal of attention is appropriately focused on childhood immunization, for every child who dies of a vaccine-preventable disease, there are 400 adults who die from vaccine-preventable diseases. The majority of such individuals visited a physician but did not receive an immunization.

Most of the needless deaths are due to pneumococcal disease and influenza. In fact, pneumonia and influenza jointly are the sixth leading cause of death in the United States. Pharmacists know many people who need pneumococcal and influenza vaccines: people 65 years of age and people with heart disease, chronic lung disease, diabetes, and other conditions. While 60% of the elderly now receive the influenza vaccine each year, less than 30% get the pneumococcal immunization.

Pharmacists have been recognized as the most accessible healthcare professionals, with the equivalent of the entire U.S. population (250 million people) visiting a pharmacy every week. Thus, pharmacists and pharmacy students have a major role to play in ensuring higher immunization rates and decreasing the incidence of vaccine-preventable diseases.

To help further address these issues, the American Pharmaceutical Association Academy of Students of Pharmacy (APhA-ASP) and the Student National Pharmaceutical Association (SNPhA) created *Operation Immunization: Pharmacy Students and Practitioners Protecting the Public Health*. This program is an immunization awareness campaign designed to increase the public's knowledge of immunizations and raise the number of adults and children receiving immunizations.

High accessibility allows pharmacists and pharmacy students to play a major role in ensuring higher immunization rates and decreasing the incidence of vaccine-preventable diseases. As of July 1999, hundreds of pharmacists in 30 states were part of the growing role pharmacists are playing as providers of immunizations.

Why Operation Immunization?

Operation Immunization is an immunization awareness campaign designed to increase the public's knowledge of immunizations and raise the number of adults and children receiving immunizations. While *Operation Immunization* occurs at the beginning of the flu season during National Pharmacy Week, it is important to keep in mind that immunizations given throughout the year are necessary. Pneumococcal disease and hepatitis B kill throughout the year. These vaccines, if given throughout the year, could prevent more than 45,000 deaths.

Operation Immunization consists of a promotional campaign designed to increase community awareness of immunization information and to advise patients where they can obtain the proper immunizations. This campaign also promotes the implementation of immunization services in pharmacies. Pharmacists practicing in states where they have authorization to immunize and have been trained to immunize patients are asked by the APhA-ASP and SNPhA chapter members to provide immunization services at their pharmacy and are encouraged to administer vaccinations as part of this campaign. In states where pharmacists are not authorized or trained to administer immunizations, opportunities exist for chapters to create partnerships with physicians, nurses, and other healthcare professionals to administer immunizations in a pharmacy. By having pharmacists administer immunizations or having the immunizations administered in a pharmacy, chapter members hope to increase the public's awareness of the important role both pharmacists and pharmacy students play in public health.

As pharmacy students and as future healthcare providers, you can show how the pharmacy profession is an excellent resource in the fight against the growing morbidity and mortality associated with vaccine-preventable diseases.

Tools that Were Used

A notebook was made available that helped student chapters implement, manage, and market an immunization advocacy campaign in their community. Included in the notebook was a time line that provided a step-by-step explanation of how to run the campaign. Promotional materials used for *Operation Immunization* were also provided for the chapters.

Results

This campaign, which began in the fall of 1997, immunized 25,000 people in 1997–98 and 53,000 people in 1998–99.

Summary

By using the suggestions in this chapter and in the rest of the book, pharmacy students can begin their interaction with the media. If you begin early in your pharmacy career, it will be easier as you enter your practice site to continue to position your pharmacy practice by using public relations.

Good luck, and have fun! ▶

Public Relations Terminology

Advertising—applies to controlled messages that appeal directly to the public (or segments of the public) from an identified organization or individual who purchases space and/or time to have it appear exactly as the originator submitted it, where, when, and how often is specified.

Communication (in the public relations context)—interchange of information; also the transaction of conveying thought from one party to another.

Community Relations—dealing and communicating with the citizens and groups within an organization's operating area.

Financial Public Relations—dealing and communicating with the shareholders of an organization and the investment community.

Government Relations—dealing and communicating with legislatures and government agencies on behalf of an organization.

Industry Relations—dealing and communicating with firms within the industry of the organization.

Issues Management—systematic identification and action regarding public policy matters of concern to an organization.

Media Relations—dealing with the communications media in seeking publicity or responding to their interest in the organization.

Minority Relations—dealing and communicating with individuals and groups in minorities.

Press Agentry—creating news events of a transient nature, often of a flighty sort.

Promotion—special activities, such as events, designed to create and stimulate interest in a person, product, organization, or cause.

Propaganda—efforts to influence the opinions of a public to propagate a doctrine.

Public Affairs—working with governments and groups that help determine public policies and legislation.

Publicity—applies to messages directed toward specific publics to further the particular interest of an organization or person through the editorial side of selected media without specific payment to that media for space and/or time. The publicist has no control over use of the material submitted, the time it will be used, where it appears, or how often.

Used with permission from the Public Relations Society of America.

Frequently Asked Questions

I live in a two-newspaper town, and one of the newspapers did a story about me several months ago. How long should I wait before trying to get publicity in the competing paper?

You don't have to wait at all. The fact that you have gotten publicity in one paper proves that you are of interest locally. You're correct in thinking that the competing paper won't want to write the exact same story about you, so start trying to interest them in a new story angle you've developed. Remember that it's mainly the columnists who want total exclusivity on their stories, and even they would be interested in hearing from you if you've got a new story angle for them.

Incidentally, if you've "created" news by sponsoring a special event, for example, you should definitely try to get publicity in both papers at the same time. You're current news. If one paper uses the story on Monday, you should still encourage the other paper to use the story later in the week.

May I send the same news release to different people at the same publication?

I would advise against this. Multiple submissions of the release may actually dampen their enthusiasm. If one reporter notes that you've sent it to someone else as well (and you should always explain if you've sent multiple copies), then that reporter may think, "Oh well, so-and-so will probably cover it…." and throw it away. Or if you should be fortunate enough to interest both reporters in the story, then you've created an internal problem for them. They have to decide who is going to do the story.

If time permits, the best way to handle this situation is to send a release to one person at a publication at a time. Then follow up with a phone call. If they aren't interested, you can then send the release to someone else.

Will buying ads help me get publicity?

Definitely not with major publications. The ad department and the editorial department operate completely independently.

Small publications will sometimes offer an editorial blurb on your practice if you buy space for an ad—you'll particularly see this arrangement where neighborhood restaurants and boutiques are concerned. However, these publications are usually very direct about what they are offering you, so it's not being used as a subtle way to trick you into buying an ad.

Less reputable publications may try to tell you that buying an ad in the newspaper or magazine will guarantee you editorial space. This isn't a particularly good practice. If you are approached on this basis, you'll just have to evaluate whether it's worth it to you.

How much business can you expect from publicity?

That's a very difficult question to answer, because there are so many variables involved. It depends on the publication and its audience as well as the type of article.

Obviously, if you're quoted in passing, you probably won't get as much business as you would if an entire article is devoted to you.

But regardless of exactly how much business a piece of publicity brings you, remember that every time you're written about or interviewed, it adds to your credibility.

Is print publicity more effective than broadcast publicity?

In general, you'll usually find that print publicity has the advantage of being something that can be saved. If a woman reads about you while commuting to work by train, she can save the article and may call you days or months later. If she's driving to work and hears an interview with you on the radio, it will be somewhat more difficult. Though she may later remember your name and what you were talking about, she probably won't have the opportunity to pull to the side of the road and write down enough information that she'll want to file it and save it for future reference.

But again, it's difficult to generalize. One pharmacist in the New York area had a nice 2½-minute segment on a TV news program devoted to her practice managing asthma patients. To her surprise, she received only one call as a result of that publicity. However, that one patient has referred several more patients with asthma and now she has a thriving asthma management practice. Though the pharmacist might have been disappointed in the number of calls, she certainly wasn't upset about the volume of referrals that resulted.

I just can't seem to get publicity in one particular publication. What can I do?

Be persistent. Try a different editor or reporter and think of new story angles for them. Getting publicity in one specific publication can take time, but you've just got to keep trying. In all likelihood, you'll be able to crack it.

In the meantime, remember the importance of building up your press clippings. Keep working at the smaller publications or those where you seem to have easier access.

What does speaking to a reporter "off the record" mean?

If you tell a reporter that something is "off the record," that means that the reporter is bound by honor not to quote you as the source. He or she may use the information directly or indirectly in the article, but your name will not be attached to it.

Except in extraordinary circumstances, try to avoid saying something that has to be "off the record." If there is something you'd prefer not to have known, it's a better idea not to discuss it at all.

A particular magazine in which I would like to get publicity usually does survey articles that include several businesses of the same type. They rarely focus on one individual business. If I send them my news release and they like it, is there a way to encourage them to profile my business rather than doing a survey article which will doubtlessly include my competitors?

You've obviously taken time to understand the needs of the magazine, and it's good that you're thinking through this problem now. And the answer to your basic question is, no, I don't think you can encourage them to change the format of the magazine for this one article.

However, there's reason to reconsider your attitude. If the magazine is a successful one, then they've probably determined that survey articles are popular with readers—that they are read and saved by a good number of people. In this case, response to the article may well be so healthy that it wouldn't hurt that much to share some of the publicity "wealth" with your competitors. Also, remember that you will benefit or may have already benefited from your competitors' efforts to gain media exposure.

Communications Guidelines:
For Elected and Appointed Representatives and APhA Staff

NOTE: If you will be speaking to the media or any other public audience in an official capacity, representing a pharmacy organization or healthcare facility, there are probably some "official" guidelines that you need to follow. The following is a sample of communications guidelines from the American Pharmaceutical Association. These address what you might need to consider before talking to the media or making a presentation as an official spokesperson on behalf of an organization. Check with your organization for its specific requirements.

Introduction

The American Pharmaceutical Association, like any association or organization, has two identities, one that is set forth in APhA's public documents—its bylaws, policy statements, and publications—and one that is reflected in the actions and the statements of the people who make up the organization—its leaders, members, and staff. As part of this latter group, you help to define APhA daily by the way you communicate with APhA's many publics, both through your words and through your actions. Accepting a leadership position automatically transforms one from a role as simply a member of the Association to that of a public figure representing the Association, and consequently an official APhA spokesperson.

The latter role is not insignificant. The image of the Association to the rest of the profession and to the public is dependent upon the public utterances of its elected and appointed leaders. Its positions on public and professional issues—no matter how well defined they may be in Association documents—largely become judged by what APhA leaders say publicly.

Because your role as an official APhA representative is critical in disseminating accurate information about the Association that clearly reflects its position, these guidelines have been developed to assist in the performance of those communications activities in which you may become involved as you carry out the duties of your position.

These guidelines are intended to assist *all* persons who serve in any capacity in which they officially represent the Association, including elected and appointed officers and representatives as well as staff.

Speeches and Official Presentations

As an official APhA representative, you may be asked to accept a speaking engagement or make some other appearance. In the case of speaking engagements, you may be assigned a specific topic to address, or you may be permitted to select your own topic. In either case, you will undoubtedly have some degree of latitude as to the content of your presentation. The Association, as a part of its overall communications strategy, would like to assure that such opportunities are used to their maximum advantage in getting APhA's message across to our members, the rest of the profession, and the public. Coordination of your presentation through APhA can help determine how it can best be used to convey messages important to the Association at that time.

Whenever possible, speeches and other presentations made by APhA representatives on behalf of the Association should be presented from a prepared text or outline. We request that such texts or outlines be submitted to APhA in advance of the presentation to allow time for the legal and policy review as desired. Not only does this procedure help to assure that the information presented is accurate and in keeping with official APhA policy, but it also permits the Association's public relations staff to respond appropriately to inquiries from the media that may be stimulated by your presentation. It further allows for distribution of printed copies of your text to other parties who may have an interest in or would benefit from the presentation, and it permits preparation of news reports of your presentation.

This procedure relates primarily to presentations dealing with APhA policies and activities. If you are presenting a continuing education program for APhA, or are making some other kind of nonpolitical and/or nonpolicy presentation, it does not apply. Nevertheless, we would appreciate it if you would submit a copy of your presentation to APhA for information and reference.

If you are speaking or making an official appearance in some non–APhA capacity, you should make clear in both pre-presentation publicity and in your introduction the exact capacity in which you are speaking or appearing and that you are not representing APhA. Even though these are not official APhA presentations, it would be helpful for APhA staff to have them in case they receive inquiries.

Dealing with the Media

Any person serving in an official APhA capacity may be approached by the media. By following certain procedures, you can help to assure that your media interaction generates the most positive results possible for the Association, as well as for yourself.

If you feel that you are unable to accurately respond to a media query, you should not hesitate to say so and to refer the reporter to a more knowledgeable source. If such a source does not come immediately to mind, the reporter should be referred to the Association's public relations staff who will put the media representative in touch with appropriate Association information sources.

You should not feel obligated to answer questions about the Association which go beyond your actual area of expertise. The Association's public relations staff can help you guide media queries to the proper source in these situations.

Even if a question does fall into your area of activity, you are under no obligation to respond on the spot if you are not comfortable with providing an answer. Offer to get back to the reporter yourself in the time you said you would, or ensure that an APhA member with the requisite expertise responds in a timely fashion. Being sensitive to reporters' deadlines helps to maintain cordial media relations.

As a general rule, don't answer questions you aren't asked. By providing a complete answer to the reporter's question, you have fulfilled your obligation. Don't volunteer any additional information unless asked. You may unwittingly open up areas of controversy, which are best kept out of the public domain. It also increases the chance of your being misquoted or your comments being taken out of context.

It is best not to make statements "off the record," for in spite of any assurances you may receive to the contrary, there can be no guarantee that the information you provide will not show up in print or be characterized as an APhA position.

If asked to appear on TV or radio programs that are scheduled in advance, if time permits consult with the APhA public relations staff if you wish to obtain staff assistance in preparing your remarks or tracking down needed background material. This will also permit staff to publicize your appearance widely, or at least to make selected persons aware of it in advance.

Media Relations as a Two-Way Process

In all cases, it is important that you inform APhA's public relations staff of any contact by the media, even if you do not respond directly. The Association maintains a complete record of all such contacts. Be sure to report the name of the media representative making the contact, the publication or organization he or she represents, the nature of the information that was being sought, and a phone number to follow up with the representative.

In addition to reporting on your personal media contacts, it would be extremely helpful if you would share with the APhA public relations staff any coverage of the Association or of pharmacy-related matters that you see in the print or electronic media. Providing clippings or information on items that appear on radio or television is helpful in maintaining APhA records of media coverage.

Dealing with Government

Just as it is important for the Association's communications efforts to be carefully coordinated, it is equally important that this principle be applied to APhA's government affairs activities. This is true whether those activities relate to Congress, the Administration, state legislators, or to regulatory agencies.

In the case of formal interaction with the government, i.e., submission of official written statements, oral presentation of comments at hearings, or official letters of comment to Congressional or regulatory bodies, a clearance process assures that all such materials receive a thorough policy, professional, and legal review. During the drafting and approval process, you may be asked to provide comments or review drafts. It is important that you respond as quickly as possible, since with rare exceptions we will usually be under severe time constraints in preparing the APhA statement.

In the course of your APhA duties you may also have occasion to interact informally with government officials. Because the Association believes that government officials should be educated about the profession on every possible occasion, these kinds of interactions are encouraged. However, it is important to observe the same kind of cautions that pertain to public addresses or dealing with the media, i.e., that they accurately reflect APhA policies, and note when you are speaking as an individual and not as an APhA representative. You may wish to ask the government affairs staff to brief you on the issue before speaking with the legislator or government agency representative. If time constraints preclude such discussions and you feel unqualified to address a particular issue or to provide specific information requested, you should not hesitate to refer the person to a knowledgeable APhA staff member.

When you have such interaction with government representatives, please be sure to let the APhA government affairs staff know with whom you spoke, including their position in the state or federal government, and the nature of your discussion with them, especially noting their comments.

Conflicts of Interest

Should you find yourself in a policy-making or representational situation where you feel a conflict of interest might exist (*or be perceived* to exist) as a result of your rendering advice or assistance in an area in which you may have a personal or business interest, you should immediately bring this perceived conflict to the attention of APhA so that a determination can be made as to how the matter can be best resolved to the satisfaction of all parties.

Moreover, all elected officials of the Association are asked to complete a disclosure statement to help ensure that they do not find themselves in the awkward position of possibly having a conflict of interest. Rules and policies concerning conflict of interest are provided to Association leaders when they take office. They are designed to help our leaders avoid any potential problems or resolve any questions that may arise.

August 1993

Code of Ethics for Pharmacists

Preamble

Pharmacists are health professionals who assist individuals in making the best use of medications. This Code, prepared and supported by pharmacists, is intended to state publicly the principles that form the fundamental basis of the roles and responsibilities of pharmacists. These principles, based on moral obligations and virtues, are established to guide pharmacists in relationships with patients, health professionals, and society.

I. A pharmacist respects the covenantal relationship between the patient and pharmacist.

Considering the patient-pharmacist relationship as a covenant means that a pharmacist has moral obligations in response to the gift of trust received from society. In return for this gift, a pharmacist promises to help individuals achieve optimum benefit from their medications, to be committed to their welfare, and to maintain their trust.

II. A pharmacist promotes the good of every patient in a caring, compassionate, and confidential manner.

A pharmacist places concern for the well-being of the patient at the center of professional practice. In doing so, a pharmacist considers needs stated by the patient as well as those defined by health science. A pharmacist is dedicated to protecting the dignity of the patient. With a caring attitude and a compassionate spirit, a pharmacist focuses on serving the patient in a private and confidential manner.

III. A pharmacist respects the autonomy and dignity of each patient.

A pharmacist promotes the right of self-determination and recognizes individual self-worth by encouraging patients to participate in decisions about their health. A pharmacist communicates with patients in terms that are understandable. In all cases, a pharmacist respects personal and cultural differences among patients.

IV. A pharmacist acts with honesty and integrity in professional relationships.

A pharmacist has a duty to tell the truth and to act with conviction of conscience. A pharmacist avoids discriminatory practices, behavior or work conditions that impair professional judgment, and actions that compromise dedication to the best interests of patients.

V. A pharmacist maintains professional competence.

A pharmacist has a duty to maintain knowledge and abilities as new medications, devices, and technologies become available and as health information advances.

VI. A pharmacist respects the values and abilities of colleagues and other health professionals.

When appropriate, a pharmacist asks for the consultation of colleagues or other health professionals or refers the patient. A pharmacist acknowledges that colleagues and other health professionals may differ in the beliefs and values they apply to the care of the patient.

VII. A pharmacist serves individual, community, and societal needs.

The primary obligation of a pharmacist is to individual patients. However, the obligations of a pharmacist may at times extend beyond the individual to the community and society. In these situations, the pharmacist recognizes the responsibilities that accompany these obligations and acts accordingly.

VIII. A pharmacist seeks justice in the distribution of health resources.

When health resources are allocated, a pharmacist is fair and equitable, balancing the needs of patients and society.

Adopted by the membership of the American Pharmaceutical Association, October 27, 1994.

National Pharmacy Organizations

Academy of Managed Care Pharmacy (AMCP)
100 N. Pitt Street, Suite 400
Alexandria, VA 22314
(800) 827-2627
www.amcp.org

American Association of Colleges of Pharmacy (AACP)
1426 Prince Street
Alexandria, VA 22314
(703) 739-2330
www.aacp.org

American Association of Pharmaceutical Scientists (AAPS)
1650 King Street
Alexandria, VA 22314
(703) 548-3000
www.aaps.org

American College of Clinical Pharmacy (ACCP)
3101 Broadway, Suite 380
Kansas City, MO 64111
(816) 531-2177
www.accp.com

American Council on Pharmaceutical Education (ACPE)
311 W. Superior Street, Suite 512
Chicago, IL 60610
(312) 664-3575
www.acpe-accredit.org

American Pharmaceutical Association (APhA)
2215 Constitution Avenue, N.W.
Washington, DC 20037
(202) 628-4410
www.aphanet.org

American Society of Consultant Pharmacists (ASCP)
1321 Duke Street
Alexandria, VA 22314
(703) 739-1300
www.ascp.com

America Society of Health-System Pharmacists (ASHP)
7272 Wisconsin Avenue
Bethesda, MD 20814
(301) 657-3000
www.ashp.org

Board of Pharmaceutical Specialties (BPS)
2215 Constitution Avenue, N.W.
Washington, DC 20037
(202) 429-7591
www.bpsweb.org

National Association of Boards of Pharmacy (NABP)
700 Busse Highway
Park Ridge, IL 60068
(847) 698-6227
www.nabp.net

National Association of Chain Drug Stores (NACDS)
413 N. Lee Street
Alexandria, VA 22314
(703) 549-3001
www.nacds.org

National Community Pharmacists Association (NCPA)
205 Daingerfield Road
Alexandria, VA 22314
(703) 683-8200
www.ncpanet.org

National Wholesale Druggists' Association (NWDA)
1821 Michael Faraday Drive, Suite 400
Reston, VA 20190
(703) 787-0000
www.nwda.org

INDEX